"With a pastor's heart, Tony  that not only instructs, but our local church—with all truth will stir your heart to pews everywhere."

WALTER R. STRICKLAND II, Assistant Professor of Systematic and Contextual Theology, Southeastern Baptist Theological Seminary

"It's fair to say that the contemporary church is doing a serious re-think about church membership. We are recognizing that we have bred a consumerism that prioritizes self-satisfaction over self-less commitment to the purposes of Christ. Merida courageously enters the re-think with a sweet spirit, reminding us that the one who invited us to take up our cross for him also called us to be responsible for his corporate body as well as our personal souls."

BRYAN CHAPELL, Stated Clerk, Presbyterian Church in America

"I pray that every Christian would love their church, and I believe this book can help us get there! Tony writes with a pastoral heart and offers extremely practical help for every one of us to grow in love. I believe the world will be changed when we all learn to heed this call."

JENNI PRICE, Women's Ministries Director,
The Grove Community Church, Riverside, California

"An excellent resource for all Christians seeking to understand the importance of being a part of a local church and the extraordinary blessings that come from being fully engaged and committed as a church member. If you're struggling to commit to a local church because of past church hurt or any other reason, I implore you to give this book a read."

DR. DOUG LOGAN, JR., President of Grimké Seminary;
Dean of Grimké Urban; Associate Director of Acts 29

"This book does what it sets out to do—to help ordinary Christians to love Jesus and his church and to know how to do it. Not only is it a tremendously enjoyable book to read but it achieves the rare blend of taking deep Bible truth and presenting it in an engaging and winsome way."

SIMON AUSTEN, Rector, St Leonard's Church, Exeter, UK

"Jesus loves his church—his bride—enough to die for her. Often we can take our church for granted, be lukewarm or lazy (going through the revolving door of church life on someone else's push). Yet to belong to the people of God is a great privilege and responsibility. Tony Merida shows us from the Bible the why and how of loving our church. His message is clear and urgent, because loving our church will have value into eternity."

AL STEWART, National Director, FIEC Australia

"The best thing I could say about this book is that I love the church more after reading it. And I'm confident you will, too. Whether you're new to a church, or you've spent your whole life in church, *Love Your Church* will help you experience the wonder of what God has designed you and me to experience as brothers and sisters in Christ."

DAVID PLATT, Lead Pastor, McLean Bible Church, Washington, D.C.;
Author, *Radical*

"Jesus is perfect—he will never let us down. The church, however, is full of people who are not perfect and will let us down. Why bother with them? It's because God is building a community of people who love him and who also love each other. Tony Merida's eight great things about being a church member reach beyond his own church and culture. So, whether your church sounds just like his or a bit different, you'll discover what church is for, why you should be part of a church, and why you will love being part of a church—God's family."

LIZ COX, Minister for Women and Community,
St Giles' Church, Derby, UK

"A great book—thoroughly biblical, honest, practical, and readable. It is very timely in its proper and elevated view of the glory of the local church. The eight main sections are worthy of thorough study and personal reflection. Read it, and get others to read it!"

TREVOR RAMSEY, President, Association of
Baptist Churches in Ireland

"The time has come for us to face the music: the church is in crisis throughout most of the Western world. I think this reveals that many people have a misunderstanding of the true nature of the church. It is time for us to recapture the New Testament's vision of Christ's church. I am happy to commend Tony Merida's timely book, which is a clarion call for us to fall back in love with Christ and his church."

DR. WINFIELD BEVINS, Director of Church Planting,
Asbury Seminary

"Not often do you find a book that is written for church members and which is both intensely practical and deeply theological. In *Love Your Church*, Merida helps you love not an idyllic church but your church."

AMBER BOWEN, Assistant Professor of Philosophy,
Redeemer University, Hamilton, Ontario, Canada

"The kind of book that I want to put into the hands of every person in our church. It reads like a conversation with a wise friend over a coffee, patiently walking us into a compelling vision of what Jesus wants our church to look like. Each chapter comes loaded with practical and easily implementable next steps."

ADAM RAMSEY, Lead Pastor, Liberti Church, Gold Coast, Australia;
Network Director, Acts 29 Australia & New Zealand;
Author, *Truth on Fire*

"Through careful biblical instruction, good humour, and rich personal experience, Tony Merida encourages the reader to want to serve the church over which Jesus is Lord—responsibly, joyfully and wholeheartedly. This is a 'must read' for every church member."

FRANK SELLAR, Minister, Bloomfield Presbyterian Church,
Northern Ireland

"This book reminds me why it was that, long before I became a pastor, I was thrilled to be a part of a local church. I commend it enthusiastically and hope that each member of my church will read, mark, inwardly digest, and live out the lessons learned."

ALISTAIR BEGG, Senior Minister, Parkside Church,
Chagrin Falls, Ohio; Author, *Brave by Faith*

"Church feels complicated these days. People wonder if it's even relevant anymore and we tend toward cynicism and individualism. In *Love Your Church* Tony Merida is like a big brother who explains what in the world the church is for. His eight reasons to love my church lifted my eyes off of myself and off the current cultural landscape and onto the beauty and wonder of God and how he designed his people to gather together with purpose, care, mission, and joy. This is a life-giving read."

JEN OSHMAN, Author, *Enough About Me*

"It's easy to say grand things about the church as an abstract concept. It's possible to propound a high view of 'the church', all the while having a relatively low view of the actual churches we go to. This book is a pastor's call to love 'the church' by loving our churches. Through eight short, punchy chapters, Tony encourages us to embrace all that God has for us in the motley crew that makes up the local church."

RORY SHINER, Senior Pastor, Providence City Church, Perth, Australia

"*Love Your Church* is biblical and engaging, but above all it is timely. Many of our normal church practices have been affected by the COVID-19 pandemic. Emerging from this period many recognise the need to recalibrate our church life according to the teaching of the New Testament. This accessible book provides a wonderfully helpful tool in that process of re-thinking and evaluating our priorities. I warmly commend it."

ANGUS MACLEAY, Rector, St Nicholas Church, Sevenoaks, Kent, UK

"Tony Merida provides a word-centred, Christ-exalting, accessible and practical GPS for every Christian to help them avoid the holes in the road and accelerate forward in ministry and mission together in the local church. I will enthusiastically hand this book out to the leaders and members of our church."

JONATHAN E. McCLAUGHLIN, Senior Pastor, Hamilton Road Baptist Church, Bangor, Northern Ireland

LOVE
YOUR
CHURCH

TONY
MERIDA

Love Your Church:
8 Great Things About Being a Church Member
© 2021 Tony Merida

Published by:
The Good Book Company

thegoodbook.com | thegoodbook.co.uk
thegoodbook.com.au | thegoodbook.co.nz | thegoodbook.co.in

Cover design by Molly von Borstel, Faceout Studio
Art direction and design by André Parker

ISBN: 9781784986087 | Printed in the UK

For Imago Dei Church

And for faithful church members around the world—
the unsung heroes who continue to bless the church
and advance Jesus' mission

CONTENTS

FOREWORD

Jesus did not come into this world merely to start a new community. He came to start a new kind of community. In a world of grandiosity and brutality, Jesus gave his very lifeblood to start a community set apart by beauty—his own beauty.

For example, his famous Beatitudes—the "ground rules" for his new community—begin this way: "Blessed are the poor in spirit, for theirs is the kingdom of heaven" (Matthew 5:3). His word "blessed" means "Congratulations!" It's a high-five. So Jesus is congratulating, high-fiving, celebrating and welcoming the poor in spirit. He looks past the big-shots, the heavy-hitters, the insiders, the cool kids. He looks to the poor, who have nothing to offer him, nothing to boast about, nothing but need—these are very ones he rejoices over and welcomes in and enriches as the heirs of his kingdom.

Who would start a think-tank with dropouts? Who would start a business with bankrupts? Who would start a bold new venture with failures? Jesus. He builds his new kind of community with sinners so bad they can't give God a single reason why he should even notice them.

He gathers into his arms those very sinners and says to them, *Congratulations! You stand to inherit everything worth having forever!*

In his new kind of community, we don't bring our strengths. We bring our needs. And he provides everything—and on terms of his grace, too. There is no room left for our swagger. All we have now, all we need, is Jesus in his all-sufficient mercy. And that surprising strategy is how his beauty enters into this world of ugliness.

Pastor Tony Merida and I deeply believe this. We are giving our lives to advancing this new kind of community that only Jesus can create. And I am glad to commend Tony's wonderful new book, *Love Your Church*. This book you are holding in your hands can powerfully enrich your experience of Jesus and his community.

I am struck by two things about Tony's book, for starters. First, the categories are magnificent. Look at the table of contents. It lists the priorities we really do want in our churches: belonging, welcoming, gathering, caring, serving, honoring, witnessing and sending. Who today is suffering from too much of these glorious realities? Too much belonging, for example? Have we nailed that one down so well that we can "move on"? And I'm struck that not one of these sacred privileges Tony commends to us is specific to one denomination or another. These aren't Baptist only or Anglican only or Presbyterian only. These heavenly powers are simply Christian. They show us where Jesus is present. We can reach for these gospel proofs without any concern that we might lose our way or go too far.

The second thing about Tony's book that jumps out at me is how he concludes each chapter. He offers us "Action Steps," to help us get traction at a practical level. We have enough theoretical Christianity already, don't we? What we need more of is real Christianity that makes a real difference. Tony's bullet points take us to that next level. As you come to the end of each chapter, why not dare to take the challenge, by God's grace and for his glory? Let's embody, in every practical way, real Jesus-created community in our churches.

But for me, the best thing about Tony's book is the overall tone of it and the impact it will surely make. This book will help us all see our churches with new eyes of expectancy and love our churches with new gladness of heart. Instead of finding fault, we will marvel at the privilege of belonging to a church where Jesus is present. If your church isn't beneath him, isn't it good enough for you? The whole outlook Tony imparts to us throughout this book is a new sense of wonder that we get to be involved in the greatest reality on the face of the earth today: the community where Jesus himself lives.

Walking into church Sunday by Sunday with this awareness living in our hearts, we can start breathing life into everyone around. And who isn't looking to die less and live more? I love how one of my heroes, Francis Schaeffer, said it decades ago:

> *"If the church is what it should be, young people will*
> *be there. But they will not just 'be there.' They will be*
> *there with the blowing of horns and the clashing of*
> *high-sounding cymbals, and they will come dancing*
> *with flowers in their hair."*
> *(The Church at the End of the Twentieth Century, p 107)*

And old people will come too. And our cities will begin to sense that Jesus himself has come to town!

Thank you, Tony, for helping us reach for that prophetic reality in every one of our churches.

Ray Ortlund, February 2021

INTRODUCTION

WHAT YOUR CHURCH IS

If you're reading this book, then I want you to know that I have an agenda: I want people to love Jesus and his church—and to know how to love their church.

That's it.

There is a plethora of books on the church, and I'm grateful for so many excellent resources. What is distinct about this little book is my attempt to speak to the "ordinary" Christian, with the aim that he or she—you—will realize the significance of the church and what role they can play in it. This is not a book for church leaders, though I hope they benefit from it; it is for anyone who wants to faithfully follow Jesus in the context of a local Christ-centered fellowship, and to enjoy making a difference as they do.

And if you are to love your church, the best place to start is by seeing what your church *is*.

ARE ALL THESE PEOPLE OUR FAMILY?

My wife and I have five adopted children: four from Ukraine and a son from Ethiopia. Joshua, our Ethiopian son, had been home with us for about four months when he experienced his first Christmas. I will never forget one particular moment that December—not only because it's a precious family memory but because it so wonderfully illustrates the nature of the church.

After being amazed by the snow in Northern Virginia, we entered the home of Joshua's new grandparents. The house was filled with family members—and it's a lively family! Joshua, who was five years old at the time, was holding my hand as he carefully observed all of these cousins, aunts, uncles, and grandparents. With the Christmas music playing, lights shining, and presents laid out under the tree (for him too!), he looked up and asked, "Papa, are all of these people our family?"

"Yes, son," I said. "All of these people are our family."

Likewise, every time we walk into our church's large or small gatherings, we can say of fellow believers, "All of these people are our family."

Some of you may be tempted to say in your (extended) family gatherings, "*Unfortunately,* all of these people are our family..." That too illustrates the church! Every church has people who are difficult to love. You may be one of them from time to time! Every church has some crazy uncles and wild brothers and sisters; for evidence that this has always been the case, just read Paul's letters to the Corinthians. But that's the church.

What Joshua was learning during his first Christmas was this lesson: *when you get adopted, you get a new family.* And the church is a family of adopted brothers and sisters (see Galatians 4 v 4-7; Romans 8 v 12-17). When we come to faith in Christ, we get not only a new relationship with our Father but new family members too (1 Timothy 3 v 15; 5 v 1-2; Galatians 6 v 10).

We are an "already-but-not-yet" community of brothers and sisters transformed by our elder Brother and King, Jesus; that is, we experience true salvation now (the "already"), but we await final and full salvation in the future (the "not yet") with all God's people throughout all of time. As an already-but-not-yet community, we show the world what our King is like, and what the kingdom to come will be like, through our shared life and our mission of word and deed in the world. Seen this way, the local church is like a little embassy of the greater kingdom of God, living under the gracious rule of Christ. We are situated outside of our homeland (as sojourners and exiles, 1 Peter 2 v 11), so our life and actions are different from others. We are here so that the outside world would look at us and see something different and ask, "You guys aren't from around here, are you?" No, we aren't. Our citizenship is in heaven, and we're waiting for our Savior to come from there to here and make all things new (Philippians 3 v 20).

When you gather in a local church to sing praise to God—Father, Son, and Spirit—and to sit under the word of God, partake in the Lord's Supper, observe a baptism, fellowship with fellow family members, and pray together, you are doing much, much more than "going to a religious meeting." You are part of something different—something glorious and something eternal. And all of it is made possible through the saving work of Christ Jesus.

The statements about the church in Scripture are stunning. For instance, in one single, awesome sentence the apostle Paul declares the vitality of the church, the familial nature of the church, and the truth proclaimed by the church: we are "the household of God, which is the church of the living God, a pillar and buttress of the truth" (1 Timothy 4 v 15). Or consider when Paul spoke to the Ephesian pastors/elders and said, "Pay careful attention to yourselves and to all the flock, in which the Holy Spirit has made you overseers, to care for *the church of God, which he obtained with his own blood*" (Acts 20 v 28, my emphasis). What a privilege to belong to God's church, which has been purchased by the atoning work of God's own beloved Son! Or consider how Jesus so identifies with his church that when Paul was persecuting the church, Jesus asked, "Why are you persecuting *me*?" (Acts 9 v 4; 22 v 7, my emphasis). In this moment, the terrorist who would become the apostle realized not only that Jesus is the living Lord, but that to persecute the church was to persecute him. That is how bound up Jesus' heart is with his church.

RESPONSIBILITIES THAT ARE PRIVILEGES

In this book, I want to draw your attention to eight key responsibilities of church members. Each responsibility is also a privilege.

In chapter one, we'll see why it is important to belong to a local church. In the next chapter, we'll see why and how to practice hospitality, welcoming all types of people into our fellowship. The importance of our worship services occupies the next chapter. Chapters 4 and 5 deal with the calling for church members to care for one another and to serve the body with the use of our spiritual gifts. Chapter 6 will outline some of the key responsibilities of pastors and describe how members should relate to pastors. Chapters 7 and 8 both deal with mission— both our individual witness and how we can impact our communities and the world as a local church.

This book is not meant merely to impart information. I hope that it changes you. So at the end of each chapter there is a brief list of "action steps," which is intended to show you what it may look like to become a church member who loves your church well in the area that we've explored in that chapter.

I want you to be thrilled about being a part of a local community of believers. And I know that many of us (whether we would say it out loud or not) are not too thrilled when it comes to being part of a church. There are a number of reasons why people aren't deeply invested in a church family. First, some have been hurt by members of a church, and some have been hurt by pastors. I grieve over these realities and desire for these individuals to receive care, healing, and restored fellowship in a faithful church family. If this book helps you with that, I'll rejoice.

Others are "pro church in theory but not in reality" Christians. They see church as something that's good if you have nothing going on during the weekend, or something that they want their kids to experience, but after they've grown up, it's sort of optional.

Many love the *idea* of the church but don't actually have fellowship with real believers in a local church. Some keep up with church news on social media, and even offer "advice" for pastors, but are "missing in action."

Some are open to learning about the importance of the church but simply haven't been taught that much about it. If that's you, then I'm glad you're reading!

Still others have been serving and loving their church for some time but are tired, due to their context, or internal problems in the church, or for some other reason. Exhausted Christians need to be reminded of the inexhaustible riches of Christ, and they need to be reminded of how significant their labors in his church are. I hope I can stir you up by way of reminder.

Then there are "church ninjas": those individuals that I see from the platform during our church services and about whom I think, "I don't know that person," "I haven't seen that person in a while," or "I need to get him/her/them connected to some other members." But by the time I get out to the lobby to meet them, they're gone! I marvel at their speed but would love to hear their stories. I assume some are interested seekers exploring the claims of Christianity. Others may be reluctant to get involved in the church because of a negative church experience in the past. Some may feel that our church could never be as great as their former church back home, so they stay distant. I guess some may not like my sermon and can't wait to leave. Maybe there are other reasons. I long for them to experience the joy of biblical community made possible through Christ Jesus.

Finally, some people really do love their church but are not quite sure *how* to love it. Some wonder, "If I'm not in ministry leadership, or in the band, or on some leadership team, what is my role?" If that's you, then I hope this book will help you catch a glimpse of what you can do through simple but meaningful acts of discipleship in and for your church.

Regardless of where you're at, we all will benefit by recapturing the New Testament's vision of Christ's church. We can all learn to love our church as Christ calls us to.

1. BELONGING

A GOSPEL-CENTERED FAMILY

As image-bearers of God, people are made for community. The triune God is a relational God, and he has created us for relationships.

Perhaps this is why so many popular television shows have to do with community. In the 80s, *Cheers* featured a group of friends who met to socialize at a local bar. Many folks can finish the theme song: "Sometimes you wanna go … where everybody knows your name." *Friends*, a show revolving around six friends who live in Manhattan, was wildly popular in the 90s. (And this show has recently witnessed a resurgence of interest among millennials and Gen-Zers.) "I'll be there for you / Cos you're there for me too" was sung by many avid followers. In the 2000s, millions became attached to the characters of the sci-fi show *Lost*, which told the story of survivors of an airplane crash, living together on a mysterious island; it, too, magnified the importance of relationships.

The popularity of social media also illustrates our longing for community. People want to be known, want to know others, and need friends. Many people have described finding a powerful sense of community in local gyms, as well. It has become more than a place to exercise. This need for community is also why our kids always wonder, "Will I meet any new friends?" at the start of each new school year. (If only they were as excited about biology!)

God has given us a need for community—and he has given us the place where that need for community is met: the church. Sin breaks fellowship with God and with others, but we are reconciled to God and one another through the gospel. God, then, establishes this unity in Christ. But we do have to maintain it (Ephesians 4 v 2). He gives us a place where we belong; now we need to commit to belonging.

Experiencing the blessing of community requires you to avoid distancing yourself from other brothers and sisters in the church, and to avoid neglecting times together (in small groups, in corporate worship, and in ongoing communication). This is what made the COVID-19 experience so challenging, and it is why churches creatively tried to keep believers connected in community and worship, albeit in less than ideal ways.

THE CHURCH FROM JESUS' PERSPECTIVE

When I began following Jesus in college, I was very involved in campus ministry and local outreach events, but actually I thought I could do more apart from the local church. I thought the church would slow me down. I was into "movements" and "events," not the church. I was aware of crazy drama in churches and wanted no part of it. I was interested in ministering to my age group (or slightly younger), not to a multigenerational group of folks. I was into the Christian subculture, not slow-plodding faithfulness in the context of the church.

Much of this was due to my shoddy understanding of the church prior to studying the Scriptures carefully. I had failed to see the church from Jesus' perspective— to understand the way the Bible describes the church. And I believe that there are many in this same position today. We cannot allow experience or preference to rule us when considering the church; we must see the church biblically. And that means seeing the church joyfully.

Belonging to a church means investing your life in a gospel-centered community of believers who joyfully serve one another and advance Jesus' mission together. Several decades ago, the great Welsh preacher D. Martyn Lloyd-Jones underscored the need for a joyful church:

> *The greatest need of the hour is a revived and joyful church … Unhappy Christians are a poor recommendation for the faith … The exuberant joy of the early Christians was one of the most potent factors in the spread of Christianity.*
>
> *(Spiritual Depression, p 5)*

The gospel should naturally lead us to "exuberant joy," as we consider what God has done for us in Christ. And it is in the context of the church that this joy is caught, experienced, and increased.

It's this joy—a Christ-centered joy experienced even in suffering—that's unique, powerful, uplifting, and attractive. This doesn't mean the church will be devoid of sorrow; it means that even in sorrow there is a well of joy from which to drink: the wells of our salvation. In hard times, we can be "sorrowful yet always rejoicing" (2 Corinthians 6 v 10).

It's a privilege to belong to the new-covenant people of God: to be part of those who have been saved through repentance and faith in Christ Jesus, who possess the indwelling Holy Spirit, who are joined in a local gathering, who assemble to hear the word preached, who engage in corporate worship, who are led by qualified pastors/ elders, and who enjoy the wonder of baptism and the Lord's Supper. It is an awesome thing to be part of those who commit to practicing the "one another"s of Scripture, and who scatter to fulfill the Great Commandment (love your neighbor) and the Great Commission (make disciples of all nations).

Both the universal church (all Christian believers in all times and places round the world) and the local church are important, and there's often an overlap between the two, but this book focuses on the local church. As Professor Gregg Allison says, the local church is "by far the most common referent in the New Testament's presentation of the church" (*Sojourners and Strangers*, p 61-62).

The word "church" (*ekklēsia*) generally means "gathering" or "assembly," but the church is more than a gathering. The church is a local community of believers who gather for worship and scatter for witness. They share life together centered on Jesus for the good of one another and for the good of the world. This idea of *community* is everywhere in the New Testament; the Bible knows nothing of "lone ranger" Christianity. I love how Titus says that Jesus "gave himself for us to redeem us from all lawlessness and to purify for himself *a people for his own possession* who are zealous for good works" (Titus 2 v 14, my emphasis). Did you catch that? He gave himself not just for me individually (though that's true!) but for us collectively, to purify a people for himself.

The letter of 1 Peter also has a strong community focus, using several images to remind believers of their communal identity with truths like "Once you were not a people, but now you are God's people" (1 Peter 2 v 10). The New Testament rejects the popular notion that "I'm a member of the universal church; I don't need to join a local, visible church." We show we are part of the universal church by identifying with a *real community of people locally*. It's like our union with Christ. We live out our spiritual union with Christ *visibly*, and we live out our union with other believers *visibly*.

While some people frown on the idea of church membership, it's important to recognize various biblical truths that speak about it. Here are some to consider: church discipline assumes that people in the church are identifiable (Matthew 18 v 15-17). When Paul says "expel the immoral brother," this instruction assumes that some people are in and some people are out (1 Corinthians 5 v 9-13). The New Testament also contains lists of members of a local church, which illustrates that people were identifiable (for example, 1 Timothy 5). In Acts we see regular counting of people (for instance Acts 2 v 41; 4:4, and in Hebrews 13 v 17 we find that overseers will give an account for the people they lead, which means they must know who they're accountable for. What's more, the metaphors for the church—stones in a temple, members of a family, citizens of a kingdom, and members of a body—all speak to this concept of membership and belonging.

There's certainly flexibility in how local churches seek to implement a healthy membership process, but the emphasis on belonging to a local fellowship is clear in the New Testament. Some churches have very clear membership structures in place (like my own local church); others have a less formalized approach. But whatever the case, every believer should make a real commitment to belong to a local church. Active belonging is the first privilege and responsibility of a church member (or, to put it another way, of every Christian), and the doorway to the others.

ELEVATING OUR CONCEPT OF THE CHURCH

Paul's letter to the Ephesians contains many significant passages about the church. They're mostly about the universal church, but many of these ideas apply to local churches also.

In Ephesians 1, Paul describes the church as the body of Christ, with Christ being the sovereign head of the church (Ephesians 1 v 21-23). In chapter 2, Paul reminds the believers (Jew and Gentile) of their prior alienation from God and his people, and of what Christ has done through the cross to reconcile them to God and to one another (2 v 11-18). Paul calls the church *fellow citizens, members of the household of God*, and *stones in God's temple,* with Jesus being the "cornerstone" (v 19-22).

In Ephesians 3, Paul prays for God to be glorified "in the church" (3 v 20-21). Then in 4 v 1-6, Paul discusses *the unity of the church*. He says the church is united by a divine calling (v 1), Christ-like conduct (v 2-3), and a common confession (v 4-6). He adds that God has given his people spiritual gifts for ministry and has given leaders to the church in order to equip the saints for service, that believers may grow into maturity (v 7-16).

In chapter 5 the inspired apostle says that Christ "loved the church [his bride] and gave himself for her" (5 v 25). The idea of "I love Jesus but not the church" is inconsistent and problematic. She's his bride; so that's like saying to my best friend, "I love you, and I am happy to hang out with you; but I have no time for your wife and would rather not have to see her or spend time with her. Does that sound ok for you?" Paul adds that Christ is sanctifying, nourishing, and cherishing the church and that he will one day present his church in complete holiness (5 v 26-29)—as William Cowper's hymn says, "Till all the ransomed church of God be saved to sin no more."

But we must not pass over Ephesians 3 v 10. The apostle tells us that the church—made up of Jewish and Gentile (non-Jewish) believers—is making known "the multi-faceted wisdom of God" to "the rulers and authorities in the heavens" (CSB). These "rulers and authorities" are probably both bad and good heavenly beings, although the apostle's particular concern in Ephesians is mainly with evil powers (see 6 v 12). The angels look on at God's gracious act of salvation—seen visibly as saved people gather together to praise their Savior and love one another—and they marvel (1 Peter 1 v 10-12), while demonic forces look on in fear and tremble. The evil forces have already been defeated at the cross, and they await their final defeat. So then, there is more going on with the church than meets the eye. If you are part of the church, then you are part of a cosmic sermon that is being preached to spiritual rulers and authorities. Every time you gather, you are making known the "multi-faceted" wisdom of God. God's grace and glory is displayed in a diverse people who have been called, redeemed, forgiven, made alive, and united in Christ.[1]

---

1 Another striking passage about the glory of the church is found in Hebrews 12 v 18-24, where the author speaks of believers joining in praise with myriads of the heavenly

OBSTACLES TO COMMUNITY

So, what is the problem with belonging? All too often, it's us. As Christians, we need to overcome at least four obstacles to live out this vision of gospel-centered, Spirit-filled community in the church.

Sensationalism. Many Christians are stuck on the dramatic. We get excited about huge conferences, someone else's pastor, or the latest controversy. Thrill-seekers simply don't find life in a local church stimulating enough to really get involved and stay involved. Caring for the elderly in a local church? Restoring a wayward member? Helping the single mom? Serving in childcare? These things don't usually excite sensationalists. But while these acts may not be sensational in many people's eyes, they would turn the world upside down if we began to live them out. What's more, the endless search for something bigger, greater, and more extraordinary is in the end exhausting. We need a renewal of Christians who are wholly committed to living out basic Christianity with their faith family.

Mysticism. When it comes to life in the Spirit, many think of mystical, miraculous, or private experiences. This is nothing new: Simeon the Stylite, the first of the "Desert Fathers," constructed a short pillar in the Syrian desert sometime around AD 423 and lived there for six years out of his desire to live in communion with God. But is that what it means to be spiritual? Being a desert hermit,

---

host; and how believers alive in this world are united to believers in heaven, all sharing a heavenly citizenship.

away from people and worldly distractions, elevated off the ground? As Phil Ryken asks, "Is there childcare in the desert?" (*Galatians*, p 243)—not everyone can go live in the desert alone, and even if they could, that's not the picture of discipleship in the context of community that we see in Scripture.

In contrast to the hermit's approach, consider the opening chapters of the book of Revelation, where we see Jesus giving his evaluation of and instruction to seven churches, or "lampstands," in modern-day Turkey. Jesus is described as "walk[ing] among the seven lampstands" (2 v 1; see also 1 v 13). Think about this: *Christ is walking among the church!* This is why I want my life intertwined with the church. This is why I refuse to give up on the church. Where is Jesus? He's among his church. He's up close and intimate with his church. He's the Shepherd, the Head, the Vine, the Foundation, and the Husband. To be best placed to experience Jesus in a deep, fresh, life-changing way, you don't need a perch in the desert; you need a pew in a church.

Idealism. In Dietrich Bonhoeffer's classic book *Life Together*, he talks about the problem of having a "wish dream" when it comes to the church. Bonhoeffer explains how idealism is the enemy of true community: "He who loves his dream of community more than the community itself becomes a destroyer of the latter, even though his personal intentions may be ever so honest and earnest and sacrificial" (p 26).

Wish dreams destroy community. Some have wish dreams related to small-group expectations, pastoral expectations, or program expectations. Real life together will involve highs, and it will involve lows; it will involve frustration, disappointment, and struggle. But by grace, we press on together as sinners redeemed by Jesus. This doesn't mean we don't work hard to make improvements in every area in the church (we do!). It means we rethink our expectations.

I often chuckle when wish dreamers say, "I wish the church could just get back to the way it was in the first century; those people had it all together." I want to ask, "Have you read the New Testament? Have you read 1 Corinthians? How about the story of Ananias and Sapphira in Acts 5? It's hard to get much earlier than that!" Letter after letter in the New Testament addresses *problems* in the church! The seven letters to the churches in Revelation contain rebukes to five of the seven churches. Pattern our church after the New Testament? Yes. But let's not pretend that churches in the first century were faultless. Let's kill this wish dream and be quicker to identify evidences of grace in the church rather than function as a church critic. Let's celebrate when the church has biblical priorities and show grace when our church may not prefer our preferences.

Individualism. Many (often without realizing it) live isolated lives, especially in the West, never experiencing the satisfying joy of biblical community. We know so many people, but we go deep with very few (if any). Technology won't give us what our hearts long for either. Technology may strengthen relationships, but it can't replace them. The COVID-19 pandemic taught us all this. After two weeks of video calls, I was sick of digital interaction. I thought about 2 John 12 during this dreadful experience: "Though I have much to write to you, I would rather not use paper and ink. Instead *I hope to come to you and talk face to face*, so that our joy may be complete" (my emphasis). John says there are limits to pen and ink (or, for us, the computer/texting/video). Emails, texts, and calls are poor substitutes for *embodied relationships*. Something is clearly lacking without face-to-face interaction. A lack of real embodied relationships will lead to a loss of joy.

It's a privilege to be in community with brothers and sisters. This has nothing to do with whether you are outgoing or shy, introverted or extroverted. It's at the heart of being a Christian. Bonhoeffer put it like this:

It is by the grace of God that a congregation is permitted to gather visibly in this world to share God's Word and sacrament. Not all Christians receive this blessing. The imprisoned, the sick, the scattered lonely, the proclaimers of the gospel in heathen lands stand alone. They know that visible fellowship is a blessing ... The physical presence of other Christians is a source of incomparable joy and strength to the believer ... The prisoner, the sick person, the Christian in exile sees in the companionship

of a fellow Christian a physical sign of the gracious
presence of the triune God … It is grace, nothing but
grace, that we are allowed to live in community with
Christian brethren. (Life Together, p 18-19)

We need each other. This doesn't mean we need to live together in a Christian commune. It doesn't mean community is easy, or that it does not sometimes feel hard. It will never be perfect in this world, but it can still be experienced in a way that is wonderful.

This doesn't mean that all of our friends should be Christians (that can't be the case if we want to be Christ's witnesses). It simply means that we fix our minds on a vision of the Spirit-filled Christian life that essentially involves being in community, and we must be committed to pursuing that.

ACTION STEPS

Based on the New Testament's perspective of the church, allow me to offer you some next steps.

- *Elevate your concept of the church.* Don't treat the church as unimportant, unnecessary, or a hindrance to doing great things for God. The church is imperfect but indispensable to faithful Christian discipleship.

- *Identify yourself with a people in a local church.* If you're a professing Christian, but not part of a local church, then realize that you're not following the New Testament pattern. Realize also that you're not helping yourself, for it is not wise or safe to be apart from accountability, discipline, and the oversight of pastoral leaders who will give an account to God (Hebrews 13 v 17).

- *If you're considering relocating, make joining a local church a priority.* Whether you are moving for work or school (or for some other reason), factor in the local church in your decision-making process. Be eager to unite with a gospel-centered, Bible-believing community.

- *Never forget that it's a privilege to belong to a local family of faith, and to be part of the larger universal church!* Locally, it's a gift to extend Christ's welcome to one another, to gather corporately for worship, to share life together, to give our time, talent, and treasure to further the gospel, and to live on mission together. Globally, it's a gift to stand together with our brothers and sisters around the globe, who confess Jesus as Lord. Eternally, it's a gift to know that we will be joined with all the redeemed from all time singing "Worthy is the Lamb."

- *Pray for your church regularly.* Don't under-estimate the importance of praying for the people of God, for its leaders, and for the advancement of the mission.

2. WELCOMING

GRACE-CENTERED HOSPITALITY

I recall an unforgettable occasion in my first pastorate in New Orleans. My text for the morning was James 2 v 1-13, about the sin of partiality (showing favoritism) and prejudice in the assembly. I asked the church, "How many of you want to grow numerically, as a church?" Hands went up. I then asked, "Wouldn't it be great to see this building full of people, to see ministries expanding, and perhaps to be able to invest in multiple church plants around the world?" "Amens" were offered up. But then I asked, "What if 75% of this growth came from non-white people?"

This question created an awkward moment. A few people cheered, many squirmed, and others snarled. I remember one person walking out the door. Others seemed to be thinking, "I hope you have a plan after this introduction, pastor."

The church was located in a diverse neighborhood, but the vast majority of the church members were white.

My burden was not only to see us grow numerically but for us to see our church reflect our neighborhood. So, I pressed further: "What if half of the pastoral team was black and/or brown? What if you were in the hospital, and a pastor of color visited you? How would you feel about that?" I finally asked, "As a church, do we really want to grow, or do we want more people that just look like us and share our interests, opinions, and class?" I could have phrased the question differently and simply asked, *Do we really want to be a truly welcoming church?*

One of my friends visited shortly after that Sunday and had the opportunity to greet a few people in our church. The members didn't know that this guest was a friend of mine, and one older gentleman told my friend, "I don't know if we're going to kill him first or if he's going to kill us first." Now, I had no desire to hurt or be hurt, but I had every desire to reflect the New Testament vision of the church made up of diverse believers in the Lord Jesus.

Prejudice and discrimination are ongoing human problems and talking about them (especially with regard to the church) often makes us very uncomfortable. But God's word addresses this issue in many ways and in many places, so God's people need to think about it. It occupies much of the background of Romans, as Paul is trying to unite Jew and Gentile Christians. After addressing this matter throughout Romans, Paul gets very practical in chapters 14 and 15, describing how the "weaker brother" (one with a sensitive conscience, predominantly Jewish) and the "stronger brother" (one with a stronger conscience, predominantly Gentile) are to relate to one another. He then says, "Therefore, welcome one another, as Christ has welcomed you, for the glory of God" (Romans 15 v 7). This is an important verse for every church member to keep in mind. We have no right to be welcomed by Jesus into his family, but, by faith in him, we have been received by him. He received us graciously, gladly, and fully. And now, as a church, we are to be a welcoming community of believers centered on the gospel.

The biblical narrative shows us both why alienation and division exist today and how Jesus came to remedy them. In creation, God made us in his image (Genesis 1 – 2). Every person of every race and background has equal value, dignity, and worth. But there has been a fall (Genesis 3). Sin has alienated us not just from God but from other people. Division and hostility now exist between races, classes, ages, and tribes. However, through Christ, we can be reconciled to God and to one another. Such unity testifies to the power of the gospel. Jesus breaks down walls, and we are meant to see the evidence of that in the local church (Ephesians 2 v 11-22)! And one day in the new creation, all things will be made new, and we will experience glorious unity amid beautiful diversity as we exalt the Savior (Revelation 5 v 9-10).

So, our great need is to apply the gospel to this problem, to live with a kingdom worldview, to remember the grace God has shown us, and to remember where history is headed. Partiality, prejudice, and tribalism are dark places, but the good news of Jesus invades the darkness.

BE KNOWN FOR DEEDS OF LOVE, NOT ACTS OF PARTIALITY

Put simply, faith in Christ and favoritism are completely incompatible. Social snobbery and faith in Christ don't mix. So, James says, "My brothers, show no partiality as you hold the faith in our Lord Jesus Christ, the Lord of glory" (James 2 v 1). The Greek word translated as "favoritism" or "partiality" or "prejudice" or "discrimination" is a fascinating one. It basically means, "to receive the face of someone." Literally, James says, "Don't receive the face": don't discriminate on the basis of external appearances (see Douglas J. Moo, *The Letter of James*, p 201).

The term is also plural, meaning that the Christian must not show any acts of favoritism regarding clothing, wealth, skin color, background, or other external aspects of a person. There are therefore many applications of this. Just to name a few specifics, we're tempted to show partiality based on *appearance, accent, age, affluence, ancestry, affinity,* or *achievement*. The human tendency is to view others as partial, but not ourselves. The reality is that we all have our blind spots. An obvious problem in the US has been racism in the church, with Sunday mornings being called "the most segregated hour in America." This is tragic and unacceptable. But I have also seen people be condescending to those who have particular "accents," as if speaking a particular way means someone is unintelligent or uneducated. I have seen multiple expressions of partiality from older Christians toward younger leaders, and from younger saints toward older ones. Often, the rich are given power in the church or their voice is heard more loudly than that of others. Sometimes people show a bias based on affinity, not wanting to belong to a small group simply because the others in the group don't share their interests.

All these differences are important in the sense that they are part of who we are, but they're not ultimate, for God looks at the heart (1 Samuel 16 v 7). The gospel message obliterates worldly assessments and any feeling of superiority of a particular social group (see Galatians 3 v 28; Acts 10 v 34-35).

How do we restrain our natural tendency toward partiality? We must keep our eyes on Jesus, whom James calls "the Lord of glory." Only Christ has all the glory. Don't idolize the affluent, the attractive, and the achievers—worship Christ. Be in awe of Jesus, the glorious one. Look at real glory—it's not in the rich, the powerful, or the popular; it's in the Lord. If you are captivated by Jesus' glory, then you won't fawn over people.

THE "SIT BY US" TEST

James shows us a single picture of what partiality can look like in the church: a non-welcoming worship service that involves snubbing the poor and favoring the wealthy in a corporate gathering. This is class discrimination—still a major problem around the world. The ushers put the man with the big ring in a good seat and the poor on the floor:

For if a man wearing a gold ring and fine clothing comes into your assembly, and a poor man in shabby clothing also comes in, and if you pay attention to the one who wears the fine clothing and say, "You sit here in a good place," while you say to the poor man, "You stand over there," or, "Sit down at my feet," have you not then made distinctions among yourselves and become judges with evil thoughts? (James 2 v 2-4)

The fact that the poor have to be told where to sit may mean that these people are "visitors." Another option could be that they are new converts. Whatever the case, such inhospitable actions violate Christ's teaching to show hospitality to the poor and needy (Luke 14 v 12-14). It's inconsistent with the nature of God, who is impartial and hospitable (see, for instance, Deuteronomy 10 v 17-19; Leviticus 19 v 15b-18, 33-34; Isaiah 55 v 1-3). James says such an unwelcoming stance is not just a flaw or a weakness; it is "evil" (James 2 v 4b).

I remember many years ago attending a church service as a youth evangelist. I had been speaking to the students on Friday and Saturday and was invited to preach to the entire congregation on Sunday morning. One young teenage girl who had grown up without attending church professed faith in Christ in our student gatherings on

Saturday. The next day, in her first time ever at a Sunday-morning gathering with the church, she was removed from her pew because two other members (who seemed frustrated by the number of students in the church) rudely told her, "You're in our seats; find another one." I was grieved by this report, as was the student minister who tried to counsel this young believer.

You likely recoil at that kind of treatment of a young Christian too. But we should ask ourselves what kind of *attitude* we have toward those of different backgrounds. Is your instinct one of "Sit by us," or "Let's go sit by them," or is it one of "I hope they sit elsewhere" or "Let's move somewhere else"? Do you joyfully move toward those who are different than you or do you shuffle quietly away?

WHY FAVORITISM IS A BIG DEAL

I have read my fair share of books about church through the years, but many neglect the problem of partiality and prejudice in the church, which is why I have placed it here in the beginning of this book. I recall holding a conference several years ago entitled "Ecclesia," and we asked the popular Christian speaker and leader Russell Moore to speak. This passage in James 2 was the passage he chose to expound. I thought, "Huh? I would have never gone to this passage first!" But I'm glad he did, as it had a tremendous impact on me and others. This subject really matters to God (because everyone made in his image matters to him), and it should matter to us!

As a good Father, God gives us reasons in Scripture, not just commands. He teaches us for our good. Through James, he outlines four compelling reasons for not discriminating in the assembly: or, to put it more positively, four motivations to be a welcoming church member.

First, *partiality doesn't reflect God's grace* (2 v 5a). James says that God actually has chosen many of the poor to become "rich in faith" (see also 1 Corinthians 1 v 26-31). This was certainly true of the early church—the gospel was exploding on the fringes of society in major cities. Around AD 178 the Greek philosopher Celsus criticized Christianity for its appeal to the common people. He mockingly wrote of Christians:

> *Let no cultured person draw near, none wise, none sensible; for all that kind of thing we count evil; but if any man is ignorant, if any is wanting in sense and culture, if any is a fool let him come boldly ... We see them in their own houses, wool dressers, cobblers and fullers, the most uneducated and vulgar persons ... [Christians are] like a swarm of bats—or ants creeping out of their nests—or frogs holding a symposium round a swamp—or worms convening in mud.*

I can imagine a pastor responding to Celsus' criticism at the next Sunday gathering: "Welcome to the worm convention, brothers and sisters."

To be clear, it's not that the rich are excluded. There are rich believers in the Bible! But you don't come to Christ "rich in spirit" or "middle-class in spirit" but "poor in spirit" (Matthew 5 v 3). Never forget that God welcomed you when you were bankrupt, having nothing to offer. Christ cleansed you and clothed you with his beautiful garments of grace. This reality should impact how you interact with others.

Second, *partiality doesn't reflect God's kingdom* (James 2 v 5b-7). Not only are many of the poor rich in faith, but they are also "heirs of the kingdom." In the kingdom of God, everything is turned upside down. God has reversed the poor Christian's status (see Luke 1 v 53). And one day, the total truth will be revealed about the most honorable of saints. There will be some surprises on the last day. We may well find that a poor custodian, or a poor farmer, or a struggling single mother receives more honor than a big-name pastor.

As we've already seen, the church is to be a little embassy of the kingdom of God. We are to show the world what the kingdom is like. It's different than this world's system. Only in the church would you have a poor person, with no formal education but mature in the faith, mentoring a brilliant doctor from a local university who just became a believer.

In James' day, the rich were mistreating poor Christians, and so James rebuked those in the church who were acting like the people of that unbelieving society instead of representing the honorable name of Jesus by honoring his people. There are many ways in which the church today can still dishonor the poor: failing to plant churches in poorer areas; relocating the church out of poorer neighborhoods; devaluing the poorer believer's opinion on various aspects of the church; failing to give attention to the poor in regard to church programming and scheduling; not giving poor believers equal opportunities for training and leadership in the church; allowing the rich to control decision-making in the church—just to name a few.

Third, *partiality doesn't reflect God's royal law of loving our neighbor as ourselves* (James 2 v 8-12). As Christians, we have a royal name, and we are to live by the King's royal law—to love our neighbor as ourselves. Jesus taught us that these neighbors include foreigners and enemies. This means we are simply utterly forbidden to discriminate against those who walk through our doors, regardless of where they're from or what they are like (v 9). Ignore this and, James says, it's a total violation of the whole law (v 10). The law is united, and everything hangs on loving God and neighbor. To not welcome and love our neighbor is offensive to God, the lawgiver (v 11).

James also wants believers to remember that we will be held accountable for our words and deeds. So, we should speak and act in view of God's judgment (v 12). Don't think that snubbing the poor (or anyone for any reason) is a small thing to God.

We will be judged "under the law of liberty" (v 12). To be clear, we are Christians not because of our performance but because of Christ's performance. There's now no condemnation for those in Christ Jesus (Romans 8 v 1). But this doesn't mean that we set the law aside. It means we have a new relationship to it. The law is no longer a threatening, confining burden. No, the will of God is now something that we joyfully pursue in the power of the Spirit. Obedience is liberating for the Christian, whereas sin is enslaving. The person to be pitied in James' example is the usher who is fawning over the rich. That person is actually enslaved! If they would practice real neighbor love, they would experience liberty. In the evil practice of slavery, it wasn't only the slaves who were enslaved. At a deeper level, the slaveowners and promoters of slavery were enslaved; they were enslaved to sin. When you live a life of obedience empowered by the gospel, you find real freedom.

Finally, *partiality doesn't reflect God's mercy toward us* (James 2 v 13). James concludes by saying, "For judgment is without mercy to one who has shown no mercy." He inverts Jesus' Beatitude—"Blessed are the merciful, for they shall receive mercy" (Matthew 5 v 7)—into its opposite: *Cursed are those who are not merciful, for they will not be shown mercy*. If James' audience remains on this path of showing partiality, then they will find at the end of their lives a judgment "without mercy," demonstrating that they never really possessed saving faith.

But... "Mercy triumphs over judgment" (James 2 v 13b). Believers' acts of mercy will mean that they are vindicated at the final judgment. God's mercy *in* them prompts acts of mercy *from* them, and they will stand in God's final judgment. You won't treat people with compassion and grace until you apply God's grace in your own heart, live with a kingdom worldview, practice real neighbor love, and reflect to others God's amazing mercy toward you. So, as ever, it all comes back to the gospel.

CHRIST'S GRACE PRODUCES A WELCOMING PEOPLE

In his commentary on Romans, Professor Michael Bird applies Paul's emphasis on unity among Jew and Gentile believers, using David Anderson's term "gracism." Bird writes:

> *Gracism means extending favor to others irrespective of color, class, or culture. Yes, I know that "gracism" sounds cornier than a cornfield in Cornville, Iowa, but it rings true. Gracism means that nobody will ever be asked to sit in the back of the church bus. Gracism means that we can never say "equal but separate." Gracism means that we deliberately desire to have multi-ethnic and interracial fellowships. Gracism means that we sinners who have been reconciled to God can now be agents of reconciliation with each other. Gracism issues forth in a radical deconstruction of all caste systems. Gracism means that grace is both preached and practiced toward others. Gracism means*

*that the most ruthless and efficient way to destroy
our tribal enemies is by making them our brothers and
sisters in Christ. (Romans, p 135)*

We can live as "gracists" because of Jesus' grace toward
us.

If we will remember where we came from spiritually,
we can be people of grace, who show gratitude toward
God and love toward others. Our proper response to the
grace shown toward us in Christ is the extension of grace
to others. Those who apply the gospel of grace deeply
in their own hearts will be a welcoming, hospitable,
grateful, generous, and joyful people.

Believers are not just one with others in creation, bearing
the *imago Dei*—the image of God. And we are not just
one in Adam, all sinners. Those realities are both true.
But as believers we are one *in Christ*. We are those who
"were once far off" but "have been brought near by the
blood of Christ" (Ephesians 2 v 13). Such unity is truly
remarkable. Jesus can unite people who shop at Walmart
and people who shop at Wholefoods. He can unite
techies and jocks, artists and politicians, introverts and
extroverts, even Yankee fans and Red Sox fans. When we
look at the world through the gospel of grace, we become
a welcoming people.

Pastor Ray Ortlund, Jr., who kindly wrote the foreword
to this book, is one of my heroes in the ministry. My
wife and I tell people often that when we grow up, we

want to be Ray and Jani Ortlund. Pastor Ray is over 70, and he radiates a contagious Christian passion. One Sunday, Pastor Ray gave a powerful "welcome" during the Sunday morning service. Several people had pointed out before how he would go out of his way to convey God's grace to people during his Sunday-morning welcome, but on one particular Sunday, his display of Christ's gentleness and love was shared on social media by his local church (Immanuel Nashville). Leaning over the pulpit and speaking with a sincere, careful, and gracious tone, he said this:

> *Welcome to church. Now here's the one thing I invite you to understand. You may have noticed when you walked in that the doors out there are painted red. That is an old Christian tradition, because we enter into the church through the blood of Christ.*
>
> *Out in that world, where we live the rest of the week, we never measure up. Our lives are never complete. We never fully belong. Then we come into the church through the finished work of Christ on the cross, and what makes the difference here—the reason why we belong [is that] we're walking into completeness already prepared. Therefore, we can be weak; we can be honest with ourselves, with one another, and with the Lord, and he says, "We belong."*
>
> *Welcome.*
>
> *So, to all who are weary and need rest...*

To all who mourn and long for comfort...

To all who fail and desire strength...

To all who sin and need a Savior...

This church opens wide her red doors in the name of Jesus, the friend of sinners.

Welcome, I'm glad you're here.
(@ImmanuelNash, accessed 2/8/21)

What a beautiful way to apply Paul's command to us to: "Welcome one another as Christ has welcomed you, for the glory of God" (Romans 15 v 7). Just imagine if that spirit were multiplied as it was lived out by millions of Christians around the world. Such grace and hospitality reflect the ministry of Jesus, who had no problem welcoming those whom others marginalized but who has a huge problem with his people ever doing the opposite.

Recipients of grace can say, "When I was hungry, Jesus satisfied me. When I was thirsty, Jesus became my living water. When I was naked, Jesus' righteousness clothed me. When I was homeless, Jesus welcomed me. When I was in prison, Jesus visited me. When I was sick, Jesus healed me. When I had no right to come to his table, Jesus made me his child, and seated me."

Since you have been so welcomed by the Lord of glory, be a church member who welcomes others, without prejudice, into your church gathering and into your home and your life.

ACTION STEPS

A welcoming church not only preaches the gospel but also conveys the relational warmth of the gospel. We have been brought into this diverse family that bears Christ's honorable name and are called to honor his name by allowing his grace and mercy to transform the way we think about ourselves and everyone else.

So then, let me encourage you to play your part in being part of a welcoming church, made up of diverse people united in the gospel. Here are some ways:

- *Reflect regularly on how Christ gently and graciously welcomed you.* Welcome others with that kind of warmth and hospitality.

- *Ask God to search your heart for any pride and prejudice that you may have.* The only thing you have to lose is the sin that entangles you; so repent and allow God to change you, making you more like Jesus.

- *In your gatherings, be on the lookout for those who are by themselves.* Author Rebecca McLaughlin offered three rules of engagement recently on social media: "(1) An alone person in our gathering is an emergency. (2) Friends can wait. (3) Introduce a newcomer to someone else. Let's all be missionaries at church today!" (@RebeccaMcLaugh, 5/5/19). Don't attend corporate worship as a consumer watching the show but as a minister eager to welcome and to bless.

- *Consider volunteering for ministries that extend hospitality.* Perhaps that's your church's greeting team, childcare team, parking-lot greeters, or ushers. Don't underestimate how important these ministries are! When you practice hospitality, you're reflecting the character of God and the storyline of Scripture, and displaying the fruit of the gospel in your heart.

- *Pray for your pastors and fellow church members: that we will truly reflect the ministry of Jesus, who is the friend of sinners.* Pray that we, who have been welcomed into his kingdom, will put his gracious hospitality on display.

3. GATHERING

VALUING THE CORPORATE MEETING

The church is more than a building you visit and more than an event you attend. However, this doesn't mean that gathering together for corporate worship is unimportant. The gathering is a big deal, for as you meet together...

> *you have come to Mount Zion and to the city of the living God, the heavenly Jerusalem, and to innumerable angels in festal gathering, and to the assembly of the firstborn who are enrolled in heaven, and to God, the judge of all, and to the spirits of the righteous made perfect, and to Jesus, the mediator of a new covenant ... let us be grateful for receiving a kingdom that cannot be shaken, and thus let us offer to God acceptable worship, with reverence and awe, for our God is a consuming fire.*
> *(Hebrews 12 v 22-24, 28-29)*

Not only is it an essential aspect of our discipleship (Hebrews 10 v 25), but it's also a foretaste of the future gathering of all God's redeemed people, giving praise to the Lamb (Revelation 5). What we do in our corporate gatherings is important for our growth in godliness, and it's an important way in which we commend the gospel to unbelievers.

Let me take you back to Acts, to a town named Troas and a memorable worship gathering:

On the first day of the week, when we were gathered together to break bread, Paul talked with [the believers], intending to depart on the next day, and he prolonged his speech until midnight. There were many lamps in the upper room where we were gathered. And a young man named Eutychus, sitting at the window, sank into a deep sleep as Paul talked still longer. And being overcome by sleep, he fell down from the third story and was taken up dead. But Paul went down and bent over him, and taking him in his arms, said, "Do not be alarmed, for his life is in him." And when Paul had gone up and had broken bread and eaten, he conversed with them a long while, until daybreak, and so departed. And they took the youth away alive, and were not a little comforted. (Acts 20 v 7-12)

The story is humorous because many of us can identify with the slow drift into sleep during a lecture, film, or (let's be honest) sermon. A pastor friend of mine once fell asleep during a prayer time at our mentor's house. And one Sunday after our worship service, an older gentleman texted me and said, "Pastor, I want to apologize for falling asleep in your sermon today. I was just really tired." He added, "I'm sure you see people falling asleep all the time during your sermons, but I'm normally awake. I was on some new medication and just couldn't stay awake. Appreciate you!" File that away in the "I don't know how to respond" category. ("Appreciate the compliment"?)

So I love the realism of this story. As a preacher myself, I've always taken encouragement from the fact that one of the greatest preachers of all time put someone to sleep! But the Troas story provides more than comedic relief; it reveals some important, timeless principles and priorities for corporate worship.

THE FIRST DAY OF THE WEEK

Luke tells us that the church met "on the first day of the week" for corporate worship (20 v 7a). Scholar F.F. Bruce comments, "The reference to meeting for the breaking of bread on 'the first day of the week' is the earliest text we have from which it may be inferred with reasonable certainty that Christians regularly came together for worship on that day" (*The Book of Acts*, p 384).

This day had been set apart by the Lord's resurrection as the Lord's Day (see Revelation 1 v 10; 1 Corinthians 16 v 1-2). Every Sunday, in a sense, is Easter Sunday for Christians. We gather to remind ourselves of the glorious fact that the tomb is empty and the throne is occupied. We remind ourselves of our living hope in our living Savior. When we observe someone being baptized, we remind ourselves of our glorious union with our risen Christ.

The way Luke describes these events in Troas gives the impression that this meeting on the first day of the week was simply the norm for churches by this time. This particular congregation in Troas met in the evenings, presumably due to work schedules and the basic way of life. Later in history, Sunday mornings became popular in parts of the world where culture and leadership were Christianized. But regardless of what time of day we meet, we should see the big idea here: meet together weekly to celebrate the glory of the risen King. There's something that's very special and significant about assembling together, celebrating the good news that Christ has died, Christ has risen, and Christ will come again.

Moreover, when we meet together for worship, we never know what might happen. Someone might fall out the window and be brought back to life! What a bummer it would have been to have been a Christian in Troas who missed the evening with Paul when one of the guys in the youth group was raised to life!

But you don't have to have some extraordinary experience every Sunday to justify making it a regular part of your life. Your habits shape you. Contrary to popular opinion, habits are not always negative. Many habits are good (like brushing your teeth!)—and assembling weekly is a good one. The author of Hebrews instructs us not to neglect meeting together "as is the habit of some" (Hebrews 10 v 25). Instead we should assemble regularly, "encouraging one another, and all the more as you see the Day drawing near." Notice that you have a role: *encouraging one another.* Rather than sitting and soaking, come ready to bless your brothers and sisters with meaningful words of encouragement. Come ready to study the Scriptures, to seek the Lord's presence, to confess sin and repent, to renew your commitment to follow Jesus, and to welcome those who are guests.

It's actually dangerous for you to not assemble regularly. The corporate assembly is one of the ways God sustains and blesses his people for long-term obedience. I sometimes meet a Christian who gathers weekly and is not thriving in their faith, but I have yet to meet a Christian who does not join the gathering and who is. So let's spend the rest of the chapter considering some of the significant aspects of corporate worship which serve to nourish our souls and to strengthen our faith.

LISTENING TO GOD'S WORD

Luke tells us that Paul spoke to the Troas church until midnight (Acts 20 v 7). In verse 11, he adds that Paul "conversed" with them until daybreak. The first part of the sermon may imply more of a dialogue, perhaps including some Q&A, whereas the latter was more of a monologue, though more free and open than a formal sermon (see Stott, *The Message of Acts*, p 321). This was a unique event, but the fact remains that the saints wanted to hear apostolic teaching (see Acts 2 v 42), and that Paul took this responsibility seriously.

Today we still gather weekly to hear God's word preached (2 Timothy 4 v 2; 1 Peter 4 v 11). Paul gave Timothy this instruction about corporate worship: "Until I come, devote yourself to the public reading of Scripture, to exhortation, to teaching" (1 Timothy 4 v 13). Notice the emphasis on the preacher's source of authority ("Scripture"), the biblical pattern of expounding Scripture ("exhortation"/"teaching"), and the significance of preaching Scripture in corporate worship ("public").

Why listen to the sermon? Because if the preacher is truly saying what God has said in his word, and declaring what God has done in his Son, then the preacher is bringing you an authoritative word, and a life-changing word of good news. The authority of the preacher doesn't come from his age or experience but from the fact that he is the one teaching from the Bible! And the life-changing power of the message doesn't emanate from the skill or charisma of the preacher ultimately, but from the Spirit applying the word to people's hearts: lives are changed through the "living and abiding word of God" (1 Peter 1 v 23).

In my office I have a replica of a Lucas Cranach painting of the German Reformer Martin Luther preaching. It shows Luther with one finger on the text of his Bible and one finger pointing to Christ, with the audience focusing on Jesus rather than on their famous preacher. It's a good picture of what should happen when we assemble. The goal of the preacher is not to give his ideas and opinions, but rather to carefully explain the meaning of a Bible text (or texts) and to exalt Jesus in his message. The late rapper Tupac used to sing "All eyes on me," but the point of a sermon is to say, "All eyes on Jesus."

In Nehemiah 8, we read of God's people experiencing what we might call a revival, as they listen to the Bible teacher Ezra explain it. The writer points out that "all the people" were "attentive" (Nehemiah 8 v 3). They weren't distracted. They were eager to learn. And as they learned, God's word impacted them. For Scripture to change you, you need to listen and understand it. Jesus taught us that how we listen is a vitally important aspect of our lives (see Mark 4 v 1-20).

Here are a few ways to sit well under the teaching of God's word:

- Listen *humbly*. Receive the word "with meekness" (James 1 v 21). This is the first key to learning Scripture: humility. We don't stand over Scripture and criticize it, but we sit under it as we allow it to confront us, instruct us, and change us.

- Listen *intently*. Fight to stay alert. Consider saying "Amen" (Nehemiah 8 v 6) when you hear something good; consider taking notes. Fight the urge to check out mentally. Remember that something supernatural and eternal is taking place.

- Listen *biblically*. Use your mind and your Bible, like the Bereans (Acts 17 v 10-15).

- Listen *personally*. Listen for yourself, not just for someone else. Don't come to critique the pastor's sermon but come ready to be addressed from God's word.

- Listen *communally*. Listen for the good of your brothers and sisters.

- Listen *obediently*. Don't merely be a receiver of the word; be prepared to be a doer of it. Listen in order to make disciples of all nations.

- Listen *practically*. Think about specific ways you should apply the message in your life.

- Listen *gratefully*. Be thankful that God speaks to his people, including you!

It's also important to get adequate rest the night before corporate worship, as Eutychus learned. Prepare for corporate worship as you would prepare for other important events. Don't let the weekly nature of this gathering detract from its importance to you and everyone else in your church family.

For many of us, the list above contained nothing new. We know these things. The question is this: do we do them?

SHARING THE FAMILY MEAL

Luke mentions the Lord's Supper—"we gathered together to break bread"—as another common event in the life of the church (Acts 20 v 7, 11—see 1 Corinthians 11 v 17-34: "when you come together"). It was probably shared in the context of a meal. The 20th-century English pastor and theologian John Stott said, "Word and sacrament [the Lord's Supper] were combined in the ministry given to the church at Troas, and the universal church has followed suit ever since" (*The Message of Acts*, p 321).

Meals are important in Scripture. In the Garden of Eden, the Lord provided for Adam and Eve. In the exodus, God provided manna from heaven and water from the rock. And where was he taking his people? To a land "flowing with milk and honey" (Exodus 3 v 17). Further, God's people were to remember their deliverance from Egypt through the Passover meal. When Christ ministered on earth, significant conversations and events often happened as he was eating with people. Following his redemptive work, he left the church with a meal by which to remember his sacrifice and his kingdom. We call this the Lord's Supper or Communion or the Eucharist. We take this meal in anticipation of the glorious feast to come (Revelation 19).

Meals have a way of taking us home. Whenever I eat meatloaf, I think of my mom because she always makes it for me when I visit. When my wife and I were in

Ukraine for forty days, we got excited when we saw the golden arches of McDonald's. We're usually not excited about McDonald's, but it was a taste from home. When we gather at the Lord's Table, we get a foretaste of home. We get to see the gospel in the Lord's Supper, to ponder God's provision, to taste Jesus' forgiveness, and to look forward to the day in which sin and sorrow are no more.

What a privilege it must have been for the apostle Paul to enjoy the Lord's Supper with these Christians in Troas: former unbelievers, now worshipers of Jesus, gathered together to taste and see that the Lord is good.

John Paton (1824–1907) took the gospel to the people of the New Hebrides islands. Some of the natives had cannibalized two missionaries twenty years prior to Paton's coming. After many trials, Paton reported the joy he experienced later when he served the first Communion to a group of new believers at Aniwa, where many eventually came to know Christ. He said:

For years we had toiled and prayed and taught for this. At the moment when I put the bread and wine into those dark hands, once stained with the blood of cannibalism but now stretched out to receive and partake the emblems and seals of the Redeemer's love, I had a foretaste of the joy of glory that well-nigh broke my heart to pieces. I shall never taste a deeper bliss till I gaze on the glorified face of Jesus himself.

(The Story of John G. Paton, Ch. LXXIII)

What a privilege to enjoy the Table with other believers. Don't ever get over the wonder of it. You may not have been a cannibal, but you were dead in your sin and unworthy to take food from this Table until God made you alive in Christ.

The Lord's Supper is powerful in its *reception*. Many Christians grow up only hearing what the Lord's Supper is not. In hearing only that side of the truth each time, they tend to have a low view of the Supper, assuming that nothing special happens when we take it. But we should experience profound delight and deep joy when we come to the Table.

The Lord's Supper is also powerful in its *proclamation*. In the Lord's Supper, the gospel is proclaimed: "Christ, our Passover Lamb, has been sacrificed" for sinners (1 Corinthians 5 v 7; 11 v 26).

Finally, the Lord's Supper is also powerful in its *unification*. In his first letter to the Corinthians, Paul speaks much about the call for unity at the Table because the "Haves" weren't treating the "Have-nots" appropriately (11 v 17–34). At the Table, we confess our unity in Christ. We are all one in Christ. We're family. There are no distinctions. This unity is also a powerful sign of what's to come. The Lord's Supper is the sign of the Messianic reign and a foretaste of the future. For, at the Table, we're proclaiming the Lord's death "until he comes" (v 26). Soon, we will feast with the King and all the redeemed (see Matthew 8 v 11).

We don't read of baptism taking place at Troas, but it's worth highlighting this other "ordinance" of the church. Baptism and the Lord's Supper are what mark off the visible church from the unbelieving world (for more on this see Mark Dever in *A Theology of the Church*, edited by Daniel Akin, p 838). Believers' baptism is administered to those who trust in Christ as Savior and Lord, and desire to publicly declare their allegiance to him by following him in the waters of baptism. Some of the most memorable Sundays in the life of our church have been when believers have read their testimonies and declare that "Jesus is Lord" before being immersed in the water and raised back up, as a picture of the believer's union with Jesus. As we say in our church, "Buried with Christ in baptism and raised to walk in the newness of life" (see Romans 6 v 1-11).

SINGING AND SPEAKING TO GOD

We should also note two other important elements in corporate worship: singing and praying. In preaching the word and preaching to the eye (through the Lord's Supper and baptism) we hear from God; in singing and praying, we speak to God.

First, singing. After Jesus instituted the Lord's Supper, Mark tells us that Jesus and the disciples "sung a hymn" before going to the Mount of Olives. Songs fill the Old Testament as the people of God sing praise to their Creator and Redeemer (for example, Exodus 15 and the Psalms). Zephaniah tells us that God sings over his people (Zephaniah 3 v 17) and in the New Testament, as his people sing back to him, there are numerous doxologies (structured statements of praise to God—for instance, Romans 11 v 33-36; 16 v 25-27; 1 Timothy 1 v 17) and early hymns (Colossians 1 v 15-20; Philippians 2 v 5-11). The last book of the Bible is filled with praises to God and to the Lamb (see Revelation 5).

Singing has always been an important aspect of the worship of God's people. It's what the liberated people of God do: sing, and sing joyfully of grace! Oppression and guilt don't evoke adoration, but grace does.

Paul gives us the following important instructions related to singing:

Be filled by the Spirit: speaking to one another in psalms, hymns, and spiritual songs, singing and making music with your heart to the Lord, giving thanks always for everything to God the Father in the name of our Lord Jesus Christ.
                                    (Ephesians 5 v 18b-20, CSB)

Let the word of Christ dwell richly among you, in all wisdom teaching and admonishing one another through psalms, hymns, and spiritual songs, singing to God with gratitude in your hearts. (Colossians 3 v 16, CSB)

Notice that both of these texts mention a rich *variety* in singing (psalms, hymns, and spiritual songs), and both emphasize the *heart*. The Ephesians passage highlights *making music*, and the Colossians text shows how singing has an important *edifying purpose*, as the truths we're singing about build us up and build up those around us. And both passages show the importance of singing to one another. Singing in corporate worship is directed to God *and* toward our brothers and sisters. Our singing should be word-centered, Christ-exalting, and community-focused.

The importance of community needs to be underscored in our day because it has become very common to have a "me and Jesus" feel in corporate singing. The lights are down in the audience, the lights on the stage are up, and no one can see anyone in the room. (At our church, *Imago Dei*, we intentionally avoid this concert feel— this individualized experience—by keeping the lights up and reminding our people to sing not only to God but to one another).

A healthy church is a singing church. The great periods of Christian history have been great eras of song production. A sign of renewal in a church is an exuberant joy in the gospel that leads to heartfelt praise.

But what if you don't feel like singing? Sometimes you may need to pause for a moment to hear your brothers and sisters singing. Sometimes you need to sing yourself out of the dumps, offering up a "sacrifice of praise to God, that is, the fruit of lips that acknowledge his name" (Hebrews 13 v 15). You need to praise God prayerfully, asking him to renew your affections. You need to sing by faith, believing the truth of what you're saying and longing for your heart to feel the wonder of that truth.

You need to sing for the sake of your struggling church family, or for your unbelieving friend who came with you.

You also need to sing to express your solidarity in the faith with your church family. That's one of the things singing does—it unites. The Boston Red Sox baseball fans have a fascinating tradition. At home games at Fenway Park, Boston fans sing "Sweet Caroline" every eighth inning. I've been in the ballpark for this experience, and no one holds back! They sing loudly and together. Your church has something greater to sing about, and a much greater unity to enjoy. So, let me encourage you, when you gather, to just let it rip! One pastor once asked, "If someone walked into your worship service and saw you singing, would they think from your singing and expression that you believe what you're declaring?" Let the answer be yes.

Then second, prayer. Prayer also fills the pages of Scripture. Our Lord taught us to pray and exemplified a praying life (for example, Matthew 6 v 9-15; Mark 1 v 35; Luke 22 v 31-32, 39-46). Throughout the book of Acts we find the church praying (see Acts 4 v 31; 12 v 5; 13 v 1-3). The apostles, too, were seriously devoted to prayer (6 v 4). Our prayers show our dependency on God. Our prayers glorify God, who is the source of all our blessings. One of the great joys of meeting together is praying together. I recently told a group of ministers, "I think I enjoy the pastoral prayer time more than preaching" (and that's saying something, because I love preaching!).

In a sermon on Paul's call for prayer in corporate worship in 1 Timothy 2 v 1-7, I remember hearing John Stott give a striking illustration. He was visiting another church, and during the prayer time there was no mention of the needs around the world. Basic local needs were noted, but nothing that expressed the church's mission around the globe. Stott warned about having a village church with a village God. We need to be a local church that has a global reach, for we have a global God who hears us and responds to his people. That means praying corporately for both local and global concerns.

A GOOD PRIORITY

During the COVID-19 pandemic, Christians were made aware of the gift of corporate worship as this privilege was taken away for a season. How many of us longed to be back together, and to enjoy the various aspects of corporate worship. I recall the first Sunday when we had people regather; our pastor for corporate worship couldn't begin the first song because he was so choked up. I missed a lot of things under stay-at-home measures (like sports and the gym!), but there was nothing I missed more than gathering with God's people for corporate worship.

However, I know not everyone felt this way. Some seemed not to miss the gathering at all, either reflecting their own spiritual condition or perhaps the state of their local church. If you are in this latter category, I have tried to highlight why the corporate gatherings are so important. It is not only right to prioritize meeting with your local church; it is good to, and exciting to. Read Hebrews 12 again and consider what is going on as you meet! Of course things will not be perfect; of course it will take an effort for us, imperfect sinners as we are, to love all that we do as we gather together. Of course there will be better Sundays and worse Sundays. But let us make sure that we are committed to prioritizing meeting together, and that our question is not "Shall we go to the church gathering?" but "How can we make the most of our church gathering?"

ACTION STEPS

Drawing on an excellent article by Gavin Ortlund,[2] let me encourage you to "make Sundays sweet" by taking the following action steps:

- *Recognize that you need your church and your church needs you.* If you are hit-or-miss on a Sunday, it will impact your spiritual health. If you're late or if you don't engage in worship, it will impact your experience. And failing to take the corporate gathering seriously doesn't help your brothers and sisters, who need your voice, your encouragement, your solidarity, your prayer, and your joy.

- *Sanctify Saturday nights.* If you have a big meeting coming up, then one thing you know to

---

2 desiringgod.org/articles/make-sundays-the-sweetest (accessed 7/2/20).

do is to get rest the night before. Athletes know that they need to prepare the day before a big event. The same is true for Sundays. Get rest on Saturday night, pray with your family, and consider reading Sunday's sermon text around the dinner table. Tomorrow is a big day!

■ *Prepare for drama at home on Sunday morning!* Drama may happen on Saturday night, but very often there are issues at home on Sunday mornings. The devil would love to make you grumpy on Sunday morning or to distract you, keeping the word from having its effect in you. Gavin Ortlund says, "So, when you climb into your minivan, tell yourself in advance, someone is probably going to spill their milk in the van, or pull their sister's hair, or chuck their Bible out the window on the interstate. When that happens, I will pray rather than yell."

■ *Have some special traditions on the day of corporate worship.* After corporate worship, consider doing something that you reserve for this special day. This may involve a particular meal, or a long nap, meals with others, or afternoon tea and reading. Look at something beautiful or enjoy God's creation on a walk, or a drive, or at a park. Whatever the case, make your day of corporate worship special and unique. Make these times so enjoyable that should you have kids, they will look back with delight on these experiences. Build holy and happy habits on the day of corporate worship.

4. CARING

DISPLAYING THE FRUIT OF THE SPIRIT

I love the movie *Remember the Titans*, a biographical sports film about the integration of black and white students at TC Williams High School in Alexandria, Virginia in 1971. The players struggle with the racial tensions of that era (tensions that still plague ours). Tempers are hot within the team, until they go away to football camp and become a family. Their coach, Herman Boone (played by Denzel Washington), requires each player to learn something about one of their teammates of another race. Eventually they're singing together in the locker room and at lunch times.

Near the end of the film, Gary (a white leader on the team) is in the hospital. Julius (one of the black leaders on the team) comes to see him, in tears. Gary's mom says, "He only wants to see you." When he enters, the nurse says, "Only kin is allowed in here." Gary responds, "Don't you see the family resemblance? That's my brother." As he and Julius chat, Julius says, "When all this is over, we gonna move in the same neighborhood together."

When the team stopped fighting with one another and became a (diverse) family, they excelled as a team. That's a good illustration of biblical community. Our enemy is not our brother or sister. We are to pull for one another, support and care for one another as family. If football can bring people together, how much more should the gospel! And this gospel unity is expressed not only in words, but through concrete actions of love.

One of the most remarked-upon aspects of the early church was how they cared for one another. If someone spied on your church today, would they remark about the same thing? Or would they say something like, "Behold, how they criticize one another!" "Behold, how they gossip about one another!" "Behold, how polite they are toward one another, but not authentically caring toward one another." There's far too much "brother-bashing" and "sister-smashing" going on today—in person and online—and there's not enough biblical "one anothering."

The "one another" passages in the New Testament demonstrate the importance of caring for our brothers and sisters in our Christian community. That there are so many of these passages illustrates that this is a non-negotiable for brothers and sisters. Consider the following (non-exhaustive) list:

- "A new commandment I give to you, that you love one another: just as I have loved you, you also are to love one another." (John 13 v 34)

- "We, though many, are ... individually members one of another." (Romans 12 v 5)

- "Love one another with brotherly affection." (Romans 12 v 10)

- "Outdo one another in showing honor." (Romans 12 v 10)

- "Instruct one another." (Romans 15 v 14)

- "Have the same care for one another." (1 Corinthians 12 v 25)

- "Through love serve one another." (Galatians 5 v 13)

- "Bear one another's burdens." (Galatians 6 v 2)

- "Bearing with one another in love." (Ephesians 4 v 2)

- "Be kind to one another." (Ephesians 4 v 32)

- "Submitting to one another out of reverence for Christ." (Ephesians 5 v 21)

- "In humility count others more significant than yourselves." (Philippians 2 v 3)

- "Do not lie to one another." (Colossians 3 v 9)

- "Encourage one another." (1 Thessalonians 4 v 18)

- "Always seek to do good to one another." (1 Thessalonians 5 v 15)

- "Let us consider how to stir up one another to love and good works." (Hebrews 10 v 24)

- "Do not speak evil against one another, brothers." (James 4 v 11)

- "Do not grumble against one another." (James 5 v 9)

- "Confess your sins to one another and pray for one another, that you may be healed." (James 5 v 16)

- "Show hospitality to one another without grumbling." (1 Peter 4 v 9)

- "Clothe yourselves, all of you, with humility toward one another." (1 Peter 5 v 5)

- "Beloved, let us love one another, for love is from God, and whoever loves has been born of God and knows God." (1 John 4 v 7)

- "No one has ever seen God; if we love one another, God abides in us." (1 John 4 v 12)

Throughout this list, you can see the call to truly care for one another. Consider reading through these verses again, and consider how you and I (and others) are missing out when we do not give and receive this kind of care. Putting them all together shows that God calls us to a high level of commitment to one another; but doing so also gives us an exciting picture of what our local churches can be, if we learn to give and receive care for one another like this.

This kind of God-honoring care is also what underlies Galatians 6 v 1-10, where we find a very helpful outline of what it looks like to care for one another. It is no accident that Paul moves from the "fruit of the Spirit" (5 v 16-24) to church care-giving (6 v 1-10). The Spirit-filled life is not so much about dramatic and miraculous power encounters or inner mystical experiences as about faithful Christians living in joyful devotion to Christ and one another. We are to display the fruit of the Spirit in the context of familial care.

GENTLE RESTORATION

"Brothers, if anyone is caught in any transgression, you who are spiritual should restore him in a spirit of gentleness" (v 1). You need a *family* to care for you spiritually. The church is "a household" (v 10) of brothers and sisters (see v 1, 18), who call God "Abba Father" (4 v 6).

Sometimes those in the family get "caught" in a "transgression" (6 v 1). The fallen need a brother or sister to come to their aid in these times: to open the trap and help set them free. They need us to do the ministry of restoration (see also James 5 v 19-20). Tim Keller points out that the term translated as "restore" was used for setting a dislocated bone into place. He then says:

A dislocated bone is extremely painful, because it is not in its designed, natural relationship to the other parts of the body. To put a bone back in place will inevitably inflict pain, but it's a healing pain. It means we are to confront, even when that will be painful, but our confronting must be aiming to prompt a change of life and heart. (Galatians For You, p 167)

We must always remember the goal of ministering to someone who has wandered off into deep sin: *restoration*. When Jesus gave the steps for church discipline in Matthew 18 v 15-17, the goal of the process was positive and constructive, as it is here: for the believer's spiritual health and well-being. Church discipline is the church's regulation of conduct among its members and leaders, achieved through counsel, correction, and, if necessary, removal from membership. Throughout the history of the church, various theologians have included church discipline as one of the key marks of the church (along with the preaching of the word and the administration of baptism and the Lord's Supper).[3]

---

3 Pastor Mark Dever writes, "Protestants have typically viewed these two marks—the preaching of the gospel and the proper administering of the sacraments—as delineating the true church over against imposters." After citing Thomas Cranmer and John Calvin as representative examples, he then adds, "A third mark of the church, right discipline, has often been added since then, though it is widely acknowledged that this is implied in the second mark—the sacraments being rightly administered." Then after citing the Belgic Confession of 1561, article 29 (which makes these three marks the marks of a true church), he summarizes with a quote from Edmund Clowney, who says that a true church includes "true preaching of the Word; proper observance of the sacraments; and faithful exercise of church discipline" (*Nine Marks of a Healthy Church*, p 8-9).

In Galatians 6, Paul does not give any steps for restoration, but he does talk about the *restorer*. The restorer should be "spiritual" (v 1). This doesn't mean perfect, and it doesn't mean we are to be the "righteousness police," but it does mean that we are to operate in the spirit of the ultimate restorer, Jesus.

Some object to this kind of one-another rebuke and restoration, seeing it as judgmental or none of anyone's business. Didn't Jesus say, "Judge not, that you be not judged" (Matthew 7 v 1)? Yes, he did—but those who appeal to this verse are often oblivious to verse 5: "You hypocrite, first take the log out of your own eye, and then you will see clearly to take the speck out of your brother's eye." In other words, once you take the log out of your eye, then you may go take out the speck in your brother's eye. Jesus isn't saying we should never be concerned for the spiritual welfare of our brother or sister! He's urging us to see to our own heart first, and then act.

But when we act, we should be *gentle*. Gentleness is a fruit of the Spirit, which implies that such a virtue happens as we abide in Jesus personally. He makes us gentle, like himself (Matthew 11 v 29). Further, the restorer should be *careful*. Paul says, "Keep watch on yourself, lest you too be tempted" (Galatians 6 v 1b). We must always be aware that we are not immune to falling ourselves. Be careful that you do not exalt yourself over your brother or sister; and be careful that you do not step into the same trap as you attempt to restore the other person.

Through the years, I have seen faithful church members do the work of restoration beautifully. Sometimes Christians drift spiritually, getting entangled in an addiction, being drawn into an unhealthy relationship, or simply being absent from gatherings. Spirit-filled Christianity looks like seeking the wayward brother or sister so that you may gently restore them. In a privatized, individualistic culture (like that of the 21st-century West), some may find this bothersome—but it's biblical Christianity. I am my brother's keeper; and I need a brother to be my keeper too!

Be ready to do the work of restoration. Don't assume others will reach out to a wayward and troubled brother or sister. Don't just hope that they will be ok. Don't leave the pastors and leaders to do this work. Care enough to take the initiative to rebuke where necessary and to pray and work for restoration whenever it's needed.

HUMBLE BURDEN BEARING

Next Paul turns to a brother or sister who is weighed down by some burden: "Bear one another's burdens, and so fulfill the law of Christ" (Galatians 6 v 2).

Here's a daily mission for all of us: be alert to the burdens of others and be committed to making them lighter. This ministry may not get a lot of public recognition, but it matters to Jesus. Paul assumes that the Galatians will have burdens, and so he exhorts the Galatians to give aid to one another.

One thing that will hinder this ministry is *pride*. "If anyone thinks he is something, when he is nothing, he deceives himself" (v 3). If I think I am above stooping to help my brother, I need to deal with my heart. Pride results in the refusal to serve the church family.

And I need to hear Paul's next words: "Let each one test his own work, and then his reason to boast will be in himself alone and not in his neighbor" (v 4). What Paul is basically saying is this: don't compare yourself to your neighbor. Instead, examine your own life in view of God's evaluation, and when you do, you will not be so prideful. Don't get puffed up because someone is sinning in a way you don't or is burdened in a way that you aren't. Paul says, *Stop feeding your pride by comparing yourself to others*.

At the same time, though, Paul wisely points out the need to differentiate between heavy *burdens* and lighter *loads*. We are to "bear one another's burdens (v 2), but at the same time "each will have to bear his own load" (v 5). Some things are too heavy to carry on our own, but other things are matters we need to take care of personally. There are legitimate and illegitimate needs. Some people treat everything as a burden, when some things are really a light load. Others treat everything like a light load, refusing to ask for help and staggering on.

So I need to take responsibility to wake up for work on time—that's my load. But if I lose my job and am in need as a result, that is a burden that may well require some help from others. Spending your money wisely is your load. Losing a loved one to cancer is a burden. The single mom with four kids has the right to expect care and help from her church.

If you are the burdened Christian, make sure someone knows about your situation. Sometimes Christians aren't aware of a brother's or sister's burdens, and that's the reason why they don't offer support. Part of being in biblical community means that we communicate with each other. It involves us being transparent enough to express to others our burden as well as humble and caring enough to help the burdened.

One of the misconceptions about pastoral care is that it is reserved only for pastors. While it's true that pastors have a special role in the church, the work of giving care is something that is to be shared by *all members*. All members can do the work of listening, caring, getting underneath the burden of others, and supporting wounded and wearied saints. In fact, one of the primary jobs of the pastor is "to equip the saints for the work of ministry" (Ephesians 4 v 12), and some of this ministry work is the work of bearing burdens and giving care. As church members we should realize that pastors are not the only ones who can care for us. The whole church is to called to give care to one another. If a church member visits you in the hospital, you shouldn't be disappointed that it wasn't the pastor! Instead, you should see this member (who is probably sacrificing time) doing Galatians-6 ministry and be thankful for it!

The climactic scene toward the end of the film of Tolkien's *The Return of the King* vividly illustrates burden bearing. Frodo is close to completing his task of dropping the evil ring in the fire. But he's too weary and worn to make it up the mountain. His loyal friend Sam says with passion, "Come, Mr. Frodo! I can't carry it for you, but I can carry you." He proceeds to help him up the mountain so Frodo can end the drama once and for all. So with us: Spirit-filled believers help their brothers and sisters carry the burdens that are crushing them.

GENEROUS SHARING

Next Paul shifts gears a bit: "One who is taught the word must share all good things with the one who teaches" (Galatians 6 v 6). He is focusing on our responsibility to share "all good things" with the one who teaches us: for a church to support its teachers materially. This would include food, money, and whatever good things are appropriate for the teacher's welfare.

Paul sometimes provided for himself to keep from burdening the church, but sometimes he did take support (see Philippians 4 v 10-20 and 2 Corinthians 11 v 8). But his principle was that it is good and right for the church to support ministers of the word (1 Corinthians 9 v 11-14; 1 Timothy 5 v 17-18). Keller comments, "We should not be consumers, who come to a church to plunder the benefits of it, without doing significant giving to that church" (*Galatians For You*, p 174).

But Paul's ultimate concern is not money; it is the furtherance of the gospel, and he knows that the God-ordained means for accomplishing this is the steady proclamation of the word of God by faithful teachers. These teachers would be limited if they themselves had to take care of their daily necessities, and so by caring for the needs of the teacher, a church says, "We want the word of God taught faithfully and effectively, so we will support you." Caring well means that we care for those who teach, and that we do so not because it's merely a "tradition" but because we love the word of God and want to see it spread to the ends of the earth.

PERSONAL HOLINESS

A Spirit-filled community also pursues holiness (that is, likeness to Jesus): "Do not be deceived: God is not mocked, for whatever one sows, that will he also reap. For the one who sows to his own flesh will from the flesh reap corruption, but the one who sows to the Spirit will from the Spirit reap eternal life" (Galatians 6 v 7-8).

Our personal lives directly impact our relational lives, and therefore one of the most important ways we contribute to the health of a local church is by practicing Spirit-filled godliness. When I seek to put sin to death in my life, it will inevitably bless others; and when I am indulging in sin, it will have a negative impact on others. We never really sin in isolation.

If you sow to the Spirit, you will reap from the Spirit. If you sow to the flesh, you reap from the flesh (5 v 16-25).

If you plant mustard seeds, don't expect peppers to grow. And if you sow to the flesh, don't expect holiness to grow.

To sow to the flesh is to pander to it, give in to it, and coddle it instead of crucifying it. The old adage is true: "sow a thought, reap an act; sow an act, reap a habit; sow a habit, reap a character; sow a character, reap a destiny" (see Stott, *The Message of Galatians*, p 170). Some Christians sow to the flesh every day and wonder why they don't reap holiness and victory and blessing.

"God is not mocked" (6 v 7). Regardless of who you are, you reap what you sow. So, choose your field wisely. Sow thoughts and deeds in the Spirit. The books you read, the people you are with, the things you do for entertainment, and the things you think are acts of sowing. Are they of the flesh or the Spirit? When you are sowing to the Spirit, you will reap the reward of the Spirit-controlled life and you will joyfully fulfill the "one anothers" of Scripture.

In *Life Together*, Bonhoeffer has a chapter entitled "The Day Alone," which comes after his chapter called "The Day with Others." He says, "Let him who cannot be alone beware of community … Let him who is not in community beware of being alone." In "The Day Alone," he stresses the need for holy habits like silence and solitude, careful Bible reading, and prayer. In other words, sow to the Spirit. These habits will inevitably bless others. Bonhoeffer says, "The day together will be unfruitful without the day alone, both for the fellowship and for the individual" (p 77, 78). Be careful to sow to the Spirit for the good of your own soul, for the good of your brothers and sisters, and for the glory of God.

PRACTICAL GOODNESS

Caring is tiring. It is a privilege and a blessing, but it is not easy. That is why Paul encourages us to "not grow weary of doing good, for in due season we will reap, if we do not give up" (v 9). Every Christian can become discouraged in doing good deeds. Paul says keep sowing. Keep loving one another. Keep resisting bickering with others. Keep rejecting false teachers. Keep bearing one another's burdens. Keep preaching the gospel, because Jesus is worth it. "As we have opportunity, let us do good to everyone, and especially to those who are of the household of faith" (v 10). Believers should be marked by practical goodness. We look for ways to show mercy "to everyone": to those around the world who have urgent needs but with a particularly careful attention on those "in the household of faith."

Here, then, is another daily mission for all of us: to look for opportunities to bless others by doing good. This will not happen by accident. It requires a sensitivity to the well-being of others. This kind of life will not happen if we are preoccupied with ourselves: preoccupation with me and care for you cannot coexist. We will not get under the burden of others, nor will we be zealous to do good, until Christ captivates our hearts and we walk by the Spirit.

Love acts. Christian love is not some abstract idea; it involves real displays of goodness, empowered by the Spirit (5 v 22). The apostle John says this about love: "By this we know love, that he laid down his life for us, and we ought to lay down our lives for the brothers" (1 John 3 v 16). The cross shows us that Christian love involves *a passion that leads to action*. Jesus didn't merely say he loved us—he demonstrated it. So, John points out, "If anyone has the world's goods and sees his brother in need, yet closes his heart against him, how does God's love abide in him? Little children, let us not love in word or talk but in deed and in truth" (v 17-18). Real love results in action and truth.

Most of us will not die in martyrdom; rather we will be called to spend our lives serving others, little by little, doing good things for our friends, neighbors, families, and church members. We will visit the sick, take groceries to an elderly couple, listen to a wounded brother, welcome a foster kid into our homes, visit a shut-in, advocate for the voiceless, take cookies to a neighbor. That may not be as "heroic" as martyrdom, but it still requires death to self, and it can all be done in the name of Jesus for the glory of Jesus.

I remember hearing a story about an inner-city pastor. A woman in the congregation said to him, "Pastor, we need to see more signs and wonders. We just haven't seen enough signs and wonders." The pastor responded, "Ma'am, over there sits a lady who has been evicted from her apartment with her children. I would consider it a sign and wonder if you would take them into your house to live for three months." There's nothing wrong with wanting to see God do extraordinary things. (I want to see that too!) But don't overlook and undervalue how the Spirit works in us to display practical love to one another. Any and every church member can and should display those signs and wonders today, in a myriad of different ways.

ACTION STEPS

This chapter only scratches the surface of what it means to care for our brothers and sisters, but hopefully it will inspire you to love your faith family in this journey of a lifetime. Here are some practical action steps:

- *Do the important work of restoring, bearing burdens, sharing, and doing good.* If someone comes to mind as you consider Galatians 6, then resolve to act on their behalf.

- *Recognize that caring for sinners and sufferers is ministry work that all believers should take part in.* Consider reading some good books on how to care for others (like *Instruments in the Redeemer's Hands* by Paul Tripp). Perhaps your church offers training on how to do basic biblical counseling; if so, take advantage of it. Look at your schedule and see if you have any margin that will allow you to do the work of listening, praying, and helping the burdened and the wayward; if not, then make some room for this important work.

■ *Remember that your personal life will always have an impact on your community, so be serious about sowing to the Spirit.* Consider adding some new "holy habits" to your life (a set time to pray, read Scripture, sing, and so on). If there are "unholy habits," resolve to put them to death! Understand that sometimes one simple change in your daily life can have a huge impact on the rest of your life and a positive impact on those around you.

■ *Look for opportunities every week to do good to others.* What might you do today? I have a friend who plans his week each Sunday evening, and that planning involves surprising people with acts of goodness. Can you imagine what would happen in your church if everyone spent time planning ways to bless each other?

■ *Pray for your church family.* Pray that it could be said of you, "Behold, how they love one another!" Pray that your church would truly care for the sick and the suffering, the weak and the wounded. Pray for yourself—because we all get weary. Ask the Lord to fill you with his Spirit so that you may put on display the fruit of the Spirit.

5. SERVING

USING THE GIFTS OF THE SPIRIT FOR THE GOOD OF THE BODY

Followers of Christ are not spectators in the church, but servants in the church. As a Christian, you shouldn't think of your church as "the place where I listen to sermons" but as "the place where I serve." To be sure, listening to sermons is important. But church members are contributors to the ministry of the church rather than consumers of that ministry—and contributing involves giving your time, talent, and treasure for the health and growth of your church.

Many Christians know that they should be actively serving in the church, but what's often lacking is deep enough *motivations* for that kind of committed, long-lasting service. So in this chapter I want to lay out three motivations from Scripture that will fire up your desire to serve, or refuel you if you are growing weary of serving: (1) God's mercy, (2) the Spirit's gifts, and (3) the Son's return. The first looks back to what God has done for us; the second reminds us that we're empowered and enabled to serve; and the third helps us to remember that our serving is not in vain! These gospel motivations provide us with a reason for serving that goes beyond "I serve because I ought to."

MOTIVATED BY THE MERCY OF GOD

As we look to the cross of Jesus, we're reminded of what God has done for us in Christ. Our sins are forgiven, we have right standing with God, and we enjoy peace with God. Such displays of God's mercy should stimulate worship and obedience.

In Romans 12, Paul magnifies God's mercy toward sinners and then proceeds to call Christians to serve God. Paul's use of "therefore" (12 v 1) signals a shift in focus and causes us to look back to the previous section in Romans 9 – 11, where Paul discusses God's gracious and merciful display of salvation in the Messiah (9 v 15-18; 10 v 11-13). It also causes us to reflect on the larger section that led up to Romans 9 – 11 (1 v 16 – 8 v 39). We are exhorted to live in view of these "mercies" of God (12 v 1): that is, to build our lives on these gospel mercies, being motivated by God's saving provision for us in Christ. It involves recognizing the power and hope that we now enjoy as the redeemed.

When we actively ponder the mercies of God in our hearts, we're inspired to commit our lives to God's worship and service (12 v 1-2). Paul says, "I appeal to you therefore, brothers, by the mercies of God, to present your bodies as a living sacrifice, holy and acceptable to God, which is your spiritual worship." The point is to give your whole self to God (6 v 13). This is our "spiritual worship" (12 v 1), which is better translated your "reasonable worship/service" or "rational worship/service." That is, when you look hard at God's mercy to you, offering yourself to him is the logical, rational, reasonable response.

The idea of a "living sacrifice" highlights an important aspect of Christian teaching. Early in Christian history, believers were accused of being atheists because they didn't have the temples, idols, or sacrifices common among the surrounding culture. Of course, we who worship the living God are not atheists, but our sacrifice is personal: we offer up *ourselves* to God in worshipful service. We worship by serving, not simply by what we do on Sundays or by singing in our services. We are called to be wholly consecrated worshipers, being committed to God in every realm of life. It's as if we're putting ourselves in the offering plate! This death to self is considered to be "holy and pleasing to God" (v 1, NIV). This is an astonishing thought: that the God of the universe is brought pleasure whenever you or I offer ourselves sacrificially in the service of his people!

Part of what it means to offer our bodies to God is explained in verse 2. There are two commands: "do not conform" and "be transformed." First, *do not allow the world to squeeze you into its mold* (as the Phillips paraphrase of the Bible puts it). We are to think differently than the outside world. Second, *be transformed by the renewing of your mind.* We're to make a break from the "mind that is set on the flesh" (8 v 7), which typifies humanity, and the debased minds of pagans (1 v 28). Our minds are to be renewed by the Spirit (7 v 6; 8 v 27). This involves giving our minds to that which is good, right and beautiful (see Philippians 4 v 8), and not returning to our old way of thinking (Ephesians 4 v 22-32). It involves filling our minds with the truth of Scripture (Colossians 3 v 16). It involves meditating on the glory of God in Christ (2 Corinthians 3 v 18).

The purpose of this transformed self and renewed mind is "that you may discern what is the good, pleasing, and perfect will of God" (Romans 12 v 2, CSB). This means we will be able to recognize and appreciate what honors God, and we can then set ourselves to obey his will.

So as you think about whether and how to serve your church, ponder the mercy of God toward you. Ponder what you deserve: judgment. Ponder what he's given you instead: salvation. This should stimulate a life of worshipful service.

MOTIVATED BY THE GIFTS OF THE SPIRIT

Paul is not done yet: "For by the grace given to me I say to everyone among you not to think of himself more highly than he ought to think, but to think with sober judgment, each according to the measure of faith that

God has assigned" (v 3). The word "for" is important because it links Paul's words here back to verse 2; the first thing Paul says after exhorting believers to have a renewed mind is to *not think too highly of yourself.*

This does not mean to be self-loathing, but rather to think with "sober judgment," meaning we should think accurately and in view of reality. Keller says:

> We need to acknowledge what we are good at and what
> we can do—because doing this makes us able to serve
> others. We are to think straight about ourselves; neither
> too low nor too high. (Romans 8 – 16 For You, p 109)

The meaning of the phrase "each according to the measure of faith that God has assigned" (12 v 3) is debated, but in my judgement the best option is to read it in light of the upcoming verses on spiritual gifts (12 v 4-8). Read this way, the phrase "measure of faith" refers to different spiritual capacities that God apportions to each person, and it is then equivalent to God's distribution of "spiritual gifts" (see Michael Bird, *Romans*, p 424). So God has given a measure of grace and faith to each member of the church. Each believer has been gifted (1 Peter 4 v 10). We should not think too highly (nor too lowly) of ourselves when it comes to these gifts, but rather be humble and faithful stewards of them.

In 1 Corinthians 12 – 14, Paul sandwiches a beautiful passage on *love* in the middle of his teaching on spiritual gifts. (1 Corinthians 13 was not, originally, written to be read out at weddings but to correct a view of our gifts that is self-promoting rather than church-serving.) In Romans 12, Paul follows his passage on spiritual gifts (v 3-8) with a section on *love* (v 9-21). And in both passages, Paul uses the metaphor of the body for the local church as he discusses the use of gifts (1 Corinthians 12 v 12-31). Christianity is communal; Christianity calls for loving service, and we are to use our gifts for the good of the body in love.

"Now as we have many parts in one body, and all the parts do not have the same function, in the same way we who are many are one body in Christ and individually members of one another" (Romans 12 v 4-5, CSB). Paul clearly loved "the body of Christ" picture of the church (see Ephesians 2 v 16; 3 v 6; 4 v 4, 25; 5 v 29; Colossians 3 v 15)—and for good reason. Just as a body has many members that each carry out important functions, so does each local church. This speaks both to our *diversity* and our *unity*. We are diverse: each member is unique and important in the body. We need hands *and* toes. We are united: we are one body in Christ. How much of your body goes to the bathroom when you need to go? All of it! We are one body.

In Romans 12, Paul mentions seven diverse spiritual gifts next (12 v 6-8). This isn't an exhaustive list of gifts but rather a list of examples. (He lists other gifts in 1 Corinthians 12 v 7-10, 28-30; Ephesians 4 v 11; 1 Peter 4 v 10.) What we should not miss in this particular list in Romans 12 is how Paul calls us to *use* our gifts with *excellence* and *passion*: "According to the grace given to us, we have different gifts: If prophecy, use it according to the proportion of one's faith; if service, use it in service; if teaching, in teaching; if exhorting, in exhortation; giving, with generosity; leading, with diligence; showing mercy, with cheerfulness" (v 6-8, CSB).

We might group these gifts in two categories: speaking gifts and serving gifts, or verbal and non-verbal gifts.[4] The speaking gifts include prophecy, teaching, exhorting, and leading (though leading also involves a lot of non-verbal serving as well as a great deal of teaching, and could be another category—but leading usually involves a great deal of teaching). The serving gifts include serving when the church is gathered and acts of mercy. This does not mean that those who speak never serve, nor does it mean that those who serve never speak! It's simply to say that these functions of word-and-deed ministry are worked out in the body through the proper exercise of individual gifts. When we use these word gifts and deed gifts, we build up the body of Christ and bring glory to God.

---

4 Another category (taken from 1 Corinthians 12) could be labeled something like "sign gifts" if we are to affirm the gifts like speaking in tongues, interpretation and miracles. For my purposes here, I just want to highlight the motivation for serving, and will confine myself to Romans 12. For an excellent study on Paul's teaching on spiritual gifts in 1 Corinthians, see D.A. Carson, *Showing the Spirit* (Baker, 1987), as well as Gordon Fee, *The First Epistle to the Corinthians* in The New International Commentary on the New Testament series (Revised edition: Eerdmans, 2014).

Speaking gifts. Teaching probably involves instruction in both formal and informal settings, for the building up of other believers. Exhorting has a range of meanings (comforting, encouraging, pleading) and may also be done in both formal and informal settings.

The most disputed of these gifts in Romans 12 is clearly prophecy. It's set apart here from teaching and exhorting so it should not be equated with preaching or teaching. Your church leadership will have a view on this, and I'm not going to try to argue for a particular position here. Without going into detail, my view is that it involves applying God's word in a more spontaneous way, directed to concrete situations.

Serving gifts. Service carries the idea of practical help for those in need. Such humble service reflects our Lord (see Mark 10 v 42-45). Those with the gift of contributing are called to exercise this gift with "generosity"—the kind of generosity that reflects the generosity of God (2 Corinthians 8 v 9). Those with the gift of leadership are to lead "with zeal." Those with the gift of mercy, who minister on behalf of the poor, weak, and hurting are to be "cheerful" in their display of mercy, instead of serving with a begrudging spirit.

Notice the spirit in which we are to use both speaking and serving gifts. Paul mentions generosity, zeal, and cheerfulness. These are the attitudes beneath these actions, for God cares about our hearts and motives and not just our external actions.

In all the detailed discussion and debate about spiritual gifts, let me underscore the obvious point here: *use your gifts passionately for the good of the body*. You need to be in a local church to be strengthened by the gifts of others, and you need to be in a local church because others need to be built up by your gifts! Gifts are not given for your own self-enjoyment or self-exaltation, or to build your platform. A Christian has no right to withhold his or her gifts from the church. God gave us these gifts because he loves the church, and we are to use our gifts for the good of our brothers and sisters.

The question is often raised, "How do I identify my gift?" And a question that's not too far behind it is "Should I only do the things which I'm particularly gifted at?" Regarding the first question, Keller points out that Paul implies at least two ways to discern your gifting (see *Romans 8 – 16 For You*, p 113-114):

1. *Self-examination.* In light of the calling to exercise "sober judgment," ask: What do I enjoy doing? Am I any good at what I enjoy? What kind of ministry is fulfilling? What problems do I most notice? What opportunities do I notice?

2. *Experience.* In light of Paul's statement about "using" your gift, realize that you need experience to know if you have certain gifts. Keller says, "It is best to try all kinds of ministry as a way to learn your spiritual 'aptitudes.'" He adds that you should study the biblical lists in

order to take an inventory and better process your experience.

The big idea is the simple and challenging truth that your gifts are not about you, but they exist for the building up of the body.

Regarding the second question, my answer is no, you don't you need to limit your service in the church to only those things that you are particularly gifted at. While serving in your gifting will bring greater fruit and joy, we shouldn't neglect other aspects of Christian service. Someone may have the gift of contribution but that doesn't mean that only those with that gift should give financially to the ministries of the church! Someone else may have a gift of teaching, but that doesn't mean they are the only ones called to make disciples by teaching (Matthew 28 v 18-20). Still another church member may not have the gift of mercy but we're still all called to show mercy (Micah 6 v 8). So, I would encourage you to be on the lookout for particular ways to use your spiritual gifts, but at the same don't be bothered if you are volunteering for service in a place where you may not be most gifted; see it as an act of loving service. Don't wait on the sidelines for the perfect opportunity to serve, but jump in and get involved.

MOTIVATED BY THE RETURN OF CHRIST

In 1 Peter 4 v 7-11, we find another important motivation for serving:

The end of all things is at hand; therefore be self-controlled and sober-minded for the sake of your prayers. Above all, keep loving one another earnestly, since love covers a multitude of sins. Show hospitality to one another without grumbling. As each has received a gift, use it to serve one another, as good stewards of God's varied grace: whoever speaks, as one who speaks oracles of God; whoever serves, as one who serves by the strength that God supplies—in order that in everything God may be glorified through Jesus Christ. To him belong glory and dominion forever and ever. Amen.

"The end is at hand"; that is, the final act of redemptive history is at our doorstep. Christ will return in all of his glory; therefore, get busy serving!

Often the anticipation of the return of Christ stimulates wild fanaticism or a drastic withdrawal from the world, but Peter doesn't mention anything extreme here. Rather, he emphasizes basic Christian living: being self-controlled and sober-minded so that we can engage in effective prayer, earnest love, gracious hospitality, and the exercise of our gifts. All of this service and speaking is done by God's strength, for God's glory.

Eschatology (our understanding of the last things) shouldn't make us fanatical but faithful. In light of Christ's return, you and I are called to be a contributing member of the church by faithfully doing works of ministry in ways that build up the body. The end is near: pray. The end is near: love one another earnestly. The end is near: practice hospitality. The end is near: serve.

Do you believe Jesus will return? Do you believe he will reward those who have faithfully served him? Then let that inspire you to serve your local church. You don't need an official position to serve. And don't limit your service to those things that are convenient, exciting, or likely to be noticed by others. Serve out of love for Christ and his people, even if that service seems mundane or trivial. When you see Christ and hear him say, "Well done, good and faithful servant," you will be glad you did!

ACTION STEPS

You have been called and gifted to serve, but how do you stay "eager to serve"? Here are some ideas to consider:

- *Dwell deeply on gospel truths to give you regular motivation.* Since faithful Christian service is motivated by theological truths (like God's mercy, the Spirit's gifting, and the Son's return), think much on God's redeeming work. Here is Keller again: "To fail to give ourselves in complete obedience to God is not only offensive morally, it is a failure to think clearly" (*Romans 8 – 16 For You*, p 107). Think regularly and thoughtfully about God's grace and mercy, and serve out of the overflow of a heart of gratitude and joy.

- *Remember that discipleship involves more than knowing things.* While maturity involves being able to articulate biblical truth, it also involves living out biblical truth. A lot of Christians know a lot of Bible verses but aren't serving anyone, and some don't even belong to a church. You grow into maturity by faithfully living out the Christian life, which involves service. This has been called the "information age," but sadly it won't be called the "application age." Don't settle for endless studies, conference, blogs, and social-media interactions. Go wash feet.

- *Use the preaching of the word and the ordinances of baptism and the Lord's Supper as ways to cultivate a heart for service.* Each time you hear the word preached, ask the Lord to convict and change you. Conviction is not a bad thing but a good thing. It's a sign of the Father's love. He doesn't discipline us with a whip but with his word. As you are convicted and challenged, repent and plan to make changes so that you may be a "doer of the word" (James 1 v 22). As you observe someone's baptism, remember your own baptism. Remember what it symbolized: the death of your old life and the arrival of the new. As you take the Lord's Supper, examine your heart, give thanks to Jesus, and be reminded of the coming kingdom; allow this sacred ordinance to give you renewed passion for service.

- *Be a servant, not a critic.* It's easy to argue and criticize. But instead, choose another path: humbly seize opportunities to serve Jesus and his people even if your service may seem small or insignificant. Welcome a new family to the fellowship, have college students in your home, give generously to the church, care for the children in the church, volunteer for student ministry, arrange chairs, play in the band, serve those who are struggling in your small group, serve the refugee family, take food to an elderly saint, or tutor a student. These are but a few examples of ways to be devoted to good works in Jesus' name. You are called and gifted to serve, but are you willing to serve the church?

- *Stay in touch with the volunteer needs of your church and offer to serve as you can.* Pay attention to announcements, church newsletters, or other forms of communication so you can know what's going on and can contribute.

- *Ask your church leaders where the particular needs are and offer to help as you can.* There may be an opportunity for you to use your gifts or to simply offer assistance to someone else.

- *Pray that you and your fellow church members will "serve the LORD with gladness!" (Psalm 100 v 2).* When my wife has a birthday and I bring her a nice gift, my response to her question, "Why did you do this?" is not "Because I had to." That doesn't honor her. The attitude that honors her is "It was my pleasure; there are none like you."[5] Likewise it is the cheerful attitude of service that shows your love for God and brings him glory, for he stands alone as being glorious and worthy of endless praise.

---

5 I have adapted this illustration from one in John Piper's *Desiring God* (Multnomah, 2011), p 94.

6. HONORING

FOLLOWING HUMBLE SHEPHERDS

Many people have a negative view toward leaders. In general, there's a lot of skepticism and criticism about them. This is especially true today in politics, but also in the worlds of business, educational institutions, families, and sports. There's a lot of distrust of leaders and a lot of hurt caused by leaders. This negativity extends to people's view of religious leaders as well. And I can sympathize with the frustration with self-serving leaders, with their leadership failures and mistreatment of others, and I grieve over the pain that some church leaders have caused and are causing.

So when this chapter speaks about honoring pastoral leaders, I can understand why you may bristle at the idea. But we must allow the Bible to shape us on this matter, as with every other matter. And this is what we see in Scripture: the presence of both bad and good leaders, and the call to honor the latter.

Paul speaks often about false teachers and corrupt leaders—for instance, he tells the Romans to "watch out for those who cause divisions and create obstacles contrary to the doctrine that you have been taught; avoid them" (Romans 16 v 17). And he also speaks often about faithful pastors and leaders (for instance, 1 Timothy 3 v 1-7; 4 v 11-16; 5 v 17). Paul was clearly aware of the fact that there were honorable leaders and dishonorable leaders (2 Timothy 2 v 20-21).

So was Peter. When Peter writes about elders/pastors/ overseers (terms which appear to be used interchangeably in the New Testament, though here we'll usually simply use the word "pastor": see Acts 20 v 17, 28; Titus 1 v 5, 7), he's not naïve. He knows that there are corrupt leaders: "False prophets also arose among the people, just as there will be false teachers among you (2 Peter 2 v 1). Don't miss this: just because corrupt leaders exist doesn't mean that the church doesn't have faithful leaders, and it doesn't mean that we shouldn't honor faithful leaders. Every member of God's flock needs a humble under-shepherd who serves under the Chief Shepherd (Jesus), and such leaders need to be respected (1 Thessalonians 5 v 12) and followed (Hebrews 13 v 7). When a faithful leader is following Jesus and being submissive to his word, then the people of God are to follow this shepherd joyfully.

HAPPY, HOLY, AND HUMBLE SHEPHERDS
What do we mean by "faithful leader"? Pastors are called to do their work willingly (1 Peter 4 v 2). They're called

to live holy lives before God—most of the pastoral qualifications are related to character, not skills (see 1 Timothy 3 v 1-7). They're called to be humble servant leaders, like Jesus (see John 13 v 1-35). To be sure, pastors aren't perfect, and they will have bad days and make mistakes, but the pursuit and pattern of a shepherd's life should be marked by happiness, holiness, and humility.

The church flourishes under such leaders, and these character traits sparkle in a world filled with fleeting pleasures, immorality, and arrogance. One such leader that embodied this life is one of my pastoral heroes, John Stott. In his book *Stott on the Christian Life*, Tim Chester tells the story of how a reporter once asked Stott, "You've had a brilliant academic career; firsts at Cambridge; rector at twenty-nine, chaplain to the Queen; what is your ambition now?" Stott replied, "To be more like Jesus" (p 225). This was more than the Sunday-school answer for Stott; it was his way of life. This was a man who often prepared his sermons on his knees with his Bible before him.

He was also a humble servant around those closest to him. René Padilla tells a story of traveling with Stott to Argentina. They arrived late at night in the pouring rain and ended up being quite muddy when arriving at their destination. The following morning Padilla awoke to find Stott cleaning Padilla's shoes! When he objected, Stott said, "My dear René, Jesus told us to wash one another's feet. Today we do not wash feet the way people did in Jesus' day, but I can clean your shoes." Stott's long-time secretary, Frances Whitehead, said, "It still amazes me that he emptied my office wastepaper basket every day for many, many years" (*Stott on the Christian Life*, p 228).

These may seem like unimpressive anecdotes, but they illustrate how Stott's private life was consistent with his public life. These kinds of stories shouldn't be surprising, but in a world of scandals such stories should encourage us. For those of us who are leaders, they challenge us. Ken Perez, who knew Stott well through the London Institute of Contemporary Christianity, said, "Some people are impressive in public but disappointing in private. John is the opposite. He is even more impressive in private than in public. His Christ-likeness, gentleness, personal kindness, and authenticity are unforgettable." Be praying that the Lord will raise up more leaders like this!

A BRIEF EXPLANATION OF PASTORING

Some view the work of a pastor as being like that of a CEO, others like that of a military general, and so on. But it is a mistake for us to take a worldly leadership category and map it onto our church. If a member (or leader) doesn't have the proper expectation of pastors, then sooner or later there will be a lot of disappointment and a lot of heartache. So, what should we actually expect from a pastor/elder/overseer? In 1 Peter 5, Peter outlines three aspects: the pastor's task, heart, and reward.

Peter describes himself as a fellow elder (1 Peter 5 v 1). A plurality of elders is normative in the New Testament (for instance, 1 Peter 5 v 5; Acts 11 v 30; 15 v 2; Titus 1 v 5), and the term refers to a role or "office": not to age but to the work of spiritual oversight. Since all church leaders are sinners, concentrating power in one person's hands carries potential for disaster—hence a church will (or should) have *elders*, plural—and those elders should not be mere "yes men." Different churches work this out differently. For instance, our church has both paid and unpaid pastors/elders (and we use both terms regularly). However your church is governed, the goal is for your shepherds to work together to help care for the flock and to empower the flock to care for each other.[6]

The task. Peter underlines the responsibility of pastors as being to "shepherd the flock of God that is among you, exercising oversight" (1 Peter 5 v 2). The job of the pastor is to tend to the sheep through careful and skillful shepherding and oversight. The idea of shepherd is a rich biblical theme providing a beautiful backdrop for pastors to understand this role. Good shepherds *know the sheep, lead the sheep, protect the sheep, and feed the sheep* (see Tim Witmer, *The Shepherd Leader*, p 189).

---

6 It's worth pointing out that Peter obviously believed in the potential for restoration of pastoral leaders who have fallen. While he was a witness to the sufferings of Jesus' life during Jesus' ministry, he denied Jesus during the crucifixion, but he experienced Christ's restoring grace and consequently had full assurance that he would be a partaker of future glory (1 Peter 5 v 1)! That's good news for all of us. While this isn't the book to comment further on restoring a leader wisely and well, we should incorporate this passage into such discussions.

The heart. Peter gives considerable space to the heart of the shepherd, pointing out some of the most prominent temptations of church leaders: they should serve "not under compulsion, but willingly, as God would have you; not for shameful gain, but eagerly; not domineering over those in your charge, but being examples to the flock" (1 Peter 5 v 2-3).

So first, pastors are not to serve out of compulsion but *willingly*. This means no one should have to beg a believer to become a pastor. This should be something that a pastor "desires" (1 Timothy 3 v 1). Additionally, pastors shouldn't begrudge the ongoing duties of a pastor: "Oh, I have to go to this elder meeting"; "I have to prepare another sermon"; "I have to make this visit."

Second, pastors are not to serve for shameful gain but *eagerly*. Faithful pastors should be motivated by the sheer love of the work. This doesn't mean pastors shouldn't be compensated (1 Timothy 5 v 17-18), but their motivation must not be one of seeking financial gain. Further, pastors shouldn't play favorites in the congregation based on the wealthiness of members. The New Testament often ties false teachers and unfaithful leaders to an unhealthy love of money (see 1 Timothy 6 v 3-5).

Finally, pastors shouldn't be domineering, but rather they should set a humble *example*. The desire for power and control often leads to toxic church environments. Christian leadership is not lordship; it's about laying down your life, humbly following Jesus, and inviting others to follow you as you follow him (see Mark 10 v 42-45; 1 Timothy 4 v 12). Leading by example is an essential aspect of pastoral leadership (see Matthew 23 v 11; Philippians 2 v 3-4, 5-8).

Domineering attitudes and actions must have no place in pastoral leadership. Pastors must not be characterized by pride, selfishness, manipulation, threats, intimidation, or structural powerplays. We should remember this when reading what Peter says about church members being "subject to elders" (1 Peter 5 v 5). He has in mind humble pastors who lead by example.

The reward. Pastors need to keep their eyes on Jesus: "When the chief Shepherd appears, you will receive the unfading crown of glory" (v 4). Jesus is the real "Senior Pastor," and he will reward the faithful service of elders. Shepherds are also sheep, and they depend upon the saving grace of Jesus Christ no less than any other church member. They, too, are looking for the glorious coming of Jesus, like every other Christian. And when Jesus returns, faithful pastors who lived out verses 2-3 will receive "the unfading crown of glory." Unlike the leafy crowns once received at Greek athletic events, here is an unfading crown of glory awarded to those who serve faithfully.

So one of the things you can do to honor your pastors is to help them keep this vision in their minds as they labor. Help them keep the wonder of our glorious hope. Sermon preparation is exhausting, lonely, and often unrewarding; pastoral care is often unnoticed and draining; but the

Chief Shepherd sees such faithful work and he will reward it. As you encourage your pastors in this way, remind yourself that Jesus sees your faithfulness as well (2 Corinthians 5 v 10; 1 Peter 1 v 9).

THE PASTOR AND YOU

The vast majority of pastors are striving to live out Peter's description of the faithful church leader in these verses. Of course they do so imperfectly—but assuming that your church's leaders are pursuing this kind of leadership, as a church member you have obligations to them.

You who are younger, be subject to the elders. Clothe yourselves, all of you, with humility toward one another, for "God opposes the proud but gives grace to the humble." (1 Peter 5 v 5)

Peter seems to be singling out those who may be less inclined to follow the elders in humility ("you who are younger"). More mature Christians will ideally have a healthy view of biblical leadership and will be committed to obeying their leaders and submitting to them, "for they are keeping watch over your souls, as those who will have to give an account. Let them do this with joy and not with groaning" (Hebrews 13 v 17). When you have faithful shepherds leading well, then you should humbly submit to their leadership. This requires an attitude of humility.

This doesn't mean that your elders are always right, or that they will always do things well and are therefore beyond correction. Peter made mistakes that required someone else to confront him and call him to repent (Galatians 2 v 11-14). In Acts 6, the apostles neglected the Greek-speaking widows in the congregation, and this needed to be brought to their attention. They didn't intend for this to happen, surely, but it did. If the apostles had weaknesses and blind spots, then I'm quite sure I do! Humility before leaders does not mean you can never question what they do: it means that when you do need to have a conversation about an issue, it's carried out humbly and biblically, not haughtily and hatefully (1 Timothy 5 v 19-20). Avoid two extremes here. Some feel that they should challenge their church leaders over everything, while others deem them as practically infallible and beyond correction. Humility navigates between the two.

In a church which is blessed by having faithful pastors who are attempting to serve under Christ in a way that honors him and builds up the body, here are five ways to respond to their leadership (I will give specific ways in the Action Step section below):

1. *Respect faithful pastors.* "We ask you, brothers, to respect those who labor among you and are over you in the Lord and admonish you, and to esteem them very highly in love because of their work" (1 Thessalonians 5 v 12-13). If you see leadership being carried out in a way that reflects biblical principles and reflects the example of Jesus, respect such leaders. The church is called to

"outdo one another in showing honor" (Romans 12 v 10), and that calling extends to honoring pastoral leaders (1 Timothy 5 v 17).

2. *Love your pastors.* "Esteem them highly *in love*" (1 Thessalonians 5 v 13, my emphasis). The honor to be given to pastors shouldn't be a distant honor but a warm honor. There should be deep affection between pastors and members (2 Corinthians 6 v 11-13). Pastors shouldn't withhold affection from members, and members shouldn't withhold affection from pastors, and all members should "love one another deeply as brothers and sisters" (Romans 12 v 10a, CSB).

3. *Follow the example of your pastors.* "Remember your leaders, those who spoke to you the word of God. Consider the outcome of their way of life, and imitate their faith" (Hebrews 13 v 7). Pastoral leaders are called to keep a close watch on both their life and their teaching (1 Timothy 4 v 16), and by doing this, the church is built up because God's people can heed God's word and follow godly examples. The idea of imitation may sound cultish, but the point isn't that a church becomes a personality cult. Rather, the idea is that you consider your leaders' conduct, love, faith, and purity, and imitate that kind of life.

4. *Be a joy to pastor.* As we saw earlier, the writer of Hebrews told those Christians to obey their

people's leaders who were keeping a watch over their souls, so that their pastors could "do this with joy and not with groaning, for that would be of no advantage to you" (Hebrews 13 v 17). Avoid being a burden to them by opposing their teaching. Avoid burdening them by refusing to attend gatherings. Avoid being quarrelsome and divisive (whether in person or online). Don't burden them by failing to contribute to the church's ministry financially. Avoid being a burden by undermining or refusing to engage in the church's mission. As they do this work, be mindful of their calling, and recognize that they seek your good and the glory of God. Let them have the joy of seeing you sitting humbly under the teaching of the word, repenting and changing as you do so.

5. *Pray for your pastors.* A careful look at the task of pastors should naturally cause us to pray for them. There isn't anything better you could do for a pastor than this. In several places we find Paul asking for the church's prayers (2 Thessalonians 3 v 1; Colossians 4 v 3-4; see also Ephesians 6 v 18-20). If the apostle needed the prayer of his churches, then your pastors certainly do! When someone asked the great 19th-century preacher C.H. Spurgeon what the secret to his effectiveness was, he said, "My people pray for me."

Every Christian needs shepherding. While it's easy to be critical toward pastoral leaders, the fact is that God has given the church leaders for the good of individual Christians, and for the building up of the body (Ephesians 4 v 11-16). As my pastor friend Thabiti Anyabwile says:

> A healthy member gives himself [or herself] to the Lord and then to the minister of the Lord, knowing that this is God's will (2 Corinthians 8 v 5) … Leadership in the local church is established by God for the blessing of his people. (What Is a Healthy Church Member?, p 97-103)

ACTION STEPS

I am personally so grateful for church members who honor me as I seek to serve them as their pastor. From my own experience, here are some specific ways to apply the previously mentioned points about how to relate to your pastors.

- *Respect your pastors by being attentive to their teaching and by refusing to participate in rumors and backbiting.* Recognize the amount of work put into sermon preparation and give honor to them by receiving God's word humbly (1 Timothy 5 v 17). Further, do what you can to end divisive gossip and petty complaints about your pastor; this honors the office and the leader, and ultimately God, who has established the structure of the church for our good.

- *Love your pastors by doing something kind for them.* Consider surprising them with a token of your appreciation (which doesn't have to be only during Pastor Appreciation month in October each year—though that's fine too!). Take note of what they like and surprise them with a token of love: perhaps a gift card, a special drink or treat, or tickets to an event. One time an elderly couple knew that my wife and I were getting out of town for a bit, and they gave us a check and told us to enjoy our time together, and that they loved us deeply. I'll never forget that. Consider helping your pastors take extended sabbaticals; these will not only bless them but the church too.

- *Express your thankfulness for your pastors teaching and example by offering words of encouragement to them.* Don't adopt the approach of "I told you 'good sermon' on your first week, and if I change my mind I'll let you know." Be consistent and thoughtful in your gratitude to God for them. You might encourage your pastor via email, a card, or a simple word of encouragement as you go out the doors each week: the more specific, the better! Those comments matter to pastors. Let them know that you appreciate them, you're for them, and you love them.

- *Be a joy to pastor by doing the little things well.* Some of these things involve showing up on time, volunteering to serve, being an encourager, avoiding gossip, watching out for the welfare of leaders and members, being generous, and maintaining a joyful attitude. I can honestly say that I have never enjoyed ministry more than I do in this current time (even though I have challenges and heartaches and sometimes wonder if I can make it to age 50), and this joy is largely due to so many people in our church who do the little things well—for, of course, these "little things" are very significant.

- *Pray for your pastors personally, with your family, and with other church members.* One of the biggest blessings I hear from some of our church members is "Our family prayed for you last night at dinner" or "Our kids prayed for you before they went to bed." Your prayers for your pastors will not only bless them, but they will bless you as well.

7. WITNESSING

DOING GOOD DEEDS AND
SHARING THE GOOD NEWS

"If you build it, they will come" is the classic line from the movie *Field of Dreams*. I like the movie; but this is a terrible evangelism strategy.

Most unbelievers have no interest in joining us this coming Sunday morning. Simply offering "a good product" isn't enough to attract people in post-Christian contexts. It doesn't matter how cool our venue is, how great the acoustics are, or how hip the pastor looks.

Those who do turn up on a Sunday are almost always there because someone brought them. Most outsiders don't wake up on a Sunday morning saying, "I bet that church has good coffee; let's check it out." Or, "I bet the music is great there, so let's go visit." Or "I hear the pastor is a funny guy; let's go have a listen." No—they say, "Let's follow through on our acceptance of that invitation our neighbor/co-worker/friend extended to come to their church with them. There's just something about the way they live, and the way their talk about their faith... let's give it a try."

As church members, each of us have to engage people in the everyday course of life—in the marketplaces, in the workplaces, in our neighborhoods, among our families, and in our recreation places. Evangelism isn't reserved for pastors or traveling evangelists—it's the responsibility of all of God's people.

THE HEART IS THE HEART OF EVANGELISM

Some believers have taken courses and read books on evangelism, memorized presentations, and more... but they still aren't engaging non-Christians. That's because evangelism is first and foremost about our hearts, not our methods. The how-to is important, but the lack of want-to is often the most obvious problem. This can creep into our hearts for a variety of reasons: lack of success in the past, the inconvenience often involved in holding out the gospel, or the fact that we run the risk of being mocked or rejected.

But the truth is that we speak out of the overflow of the heart. When a young woman gets engaged, it's amazing how her life and conversations change. She shows off that ring. She shows pictures of her fiancé. She updates her Facebook status. She begins planning the wedding. She starts shopping for that wedding dress! *Why?* She has a new love! She doesn't go days and weeks without talking about Mr. Right. She doesn't have to be forced or guilted into talking about him. She wants to. Guilt won't motivate, but beauty will; hope will; love will; awe will. We talk about that which we love, treasure, revere, and hope in.

This is Peter's point in his key passage on the heart of evangelism—1 Peter 3 v 13-17:

> *Now who is there to harm you if you are zealous*
> *for what is good? But even if you should suffer for*
> *righteousness' sake, you will be blessed. Have no fear*
> *of them, nor be troubled, but in your hearts honor*
> *Christ the Lord as holy, always being prepared to make*
> *a defense to anyone who asks you for a reason for*
> *the hope that is in you; yet do it with gentleness and*
> *respect, having a good conscience, so that, when you are*
> *slandered, those who revile your good behavior in Christ*
> *may be put to shame. For it is better to suffer for doing*
> *good, if that should be God's will, than for doing evil.*

Notice the focus on the interior life of the Christian. When you set apart Christ as holy in your heart, then your interests and conversations will change. When you treasure Jesus deeply, you will share the hope within you freely.

The context in which Peter's audience lived was characterized by a hostility to the gospel; Peter was writing to scattered Christians throughout what is now modern-day Turkey who were facing slander, ridicule, and marginalization, and would eventually also face physical persecution.

I am in Raleigh, North Carolina, and I wouldn't label my local context as hostile to the gospel but rather as being *hardened* to the gospel and *happy without* the gospel. Our local context has a lot of unchurched people (those who have grown up their whole lives essentially without the church and have no interest in it) and a lot of "dechurched" people (those who have been fringe churchgoers in the past but no longer attend). This brings its own challenges in bearing witness in today's culture.

So how shall we engage those in our context? How shall we cultivate a heart for sharing the hope of Christ? Though Peter's context was different than ours is, he gives us three timeless priorities for faithful witnesses everywhere and in every age: practical goodness, Christ-centered reverence, and daily readiness. If we can cultivate this kind of attitude and passion, then we can see fruit in our ministry to the people in our networks.

GOODNESS PROMPTS QUESTIONS

Peter repeatedly emphasizes the importance of "doing good" in his first epistle (3 v 13, 16-18; see also 2 v 12, 20; 3 v 1). Our witness involves more than good deeds, but it definitely *includes* good deeds (Matthew 5 v 16). The Great Commandment (love God and neighbor) and the Great Commission (make disciples of all nations) are not at odds. They represent what we could call the "integrative model" of mission—proclaiming good news and doing good deeds.

In our present cultural moment, everyone seems to want to be on the right side of an issue. These are volatile times, and social media makes things worse in enabling and encouraging people to rant about their opinions on all things political and cultural. But what Peter emphasizes isn't political agitation or argumentation, but rather living a beautiful life that demonstrates the fruit of the gospel in our lives. I don't mean to suggest that we shouldn't have political opinions or discuss cultural matters, but in our present culture we need to notice that Peter's emphasis is on living a life of good deeds before a watching world. This can be quite compelling.

To be a faithful witness among those in your networks, live in ardent pursuit of a virtuous life. This isn't easy, and it comes with the possibility of opposition from unbelievers (1 Peter 3 v 13-14). But ultimately God is with us, God is pleased with this conduct, and many people may be drawn to ask questions about the hope within us.

Many Christians have been trained to answer some of the basic questions that people might ask about our faith, and that's wonderful; but they don't know how to get that conversation started! Here's Peter's model: bless and do good to people. Live an attractive life under the lordship of Christ that provokes questions.

The fruit of the Spirit displayed in our practical actions in life can make a tremendous impact on a watching world. It's interesting how a joyful, gentle, loving, and peaceful person really stands out today. Let's devote our lives to putting on display the goodness of Jesus in practical acts of service to our neighbors.

REDIRECT YOUR FEAR

Fear will keep you from being a faithful witness. It can prevent you from serving someone, giving a book to someone, inviting someone to a meal, or from going in deep on the gospel. This is why Peter urges Christians to "have no fear of them" (v 14).

The fear of others enslaves us, traps us, and constrains our thoughts and actions. The writer of Proverbs says, "The fear of man lays a snare" (Proverbs 29 v 25). How do you avoid this? Peter says you avoid it by revering Jesus more than people: "Have no fear of them, nor be troubled, *but in your hearts honor Christ the Lord as holy*, always being prepared to make a defense to anyone who asks you for a reason for the hope that is in you; yet do it with gentleness and respect (1 Peter 3 v 14-15, my emphasis). Set apart Christ the Lord as holy. Be awed by Christ.

Redirect your fear—remember the holiness and glory of Jesus and you will keep others in their proper perspective. It's awe of Jesus that makes us a witness for Jesus. Living with gospel intentionality means that we don't live with a spirit of fear, but rather with a humble confidence in the Lord's presence and a humble reverence before the Lord's holiness. It's out of this heart that we will engage our unbelieving friends and family with the gospel.

READY ALWAYS AND WITH ANYONE

Two key words in this passage are easy to miss: "always" and "anyone": Peter wants us to "always [be] prepared to make a defense to anyone who asks you for a reason for the hope that is in you" (v 15). Peter is saying, *Be ready at all times to respond to every kind of person in your networks.*

Readiness means that we have to put away excuses for our lack of engagement with unbelievers. We need to accept the fact that it's never really a perfect day for evangelism. We can always find an excuse: "I didn't sleep well." "I got in an argument with my spouse." "This pollen is killing me." But everyday evangelism says, "Game on."

In coaching baseball, I'm always telling players to get in their "ready position." Why? Because some kids are out picking flowers in the outfield! One of my players got picked off first base because he was watching an airplane fly over his head. Have a heart that says "Game on"—be alert and ready to share your hope.

Here is our subject: hope. The word "defense" is the Greek word *apologia*, from which we get "apologetics." In one sense, this does demand some level of study because giving a "reason" calls for logical thought. But Peter doesn't have formal or academic apologetics in mind. He's not thinking about sophisticated answers for the existence of God, the problem of evil, and so on, in some kind of public debate. What he has in mind are ordinary conversations about our hope.

Every Christian can participate in evangelism because every Christian possesses a living hope (1 v 3). Peter doesn't tell us to "defend the faith" (though we should), but to defend our "hope." Hope, in the New Testament, is not wishful thinking ("I hope the Pelicans win the NBA title"); Christian hope is "thumbs up," not "fingers crossed." It's a settled confidence in future glory. This hope energizes our lives now, especially in suffering, and this hope shines in a hopeless world. This hope is so rare that some people will ask you about it, particularly when they are going through suffering or when they see you suffering with confidence.

This is liberating in many ways because some of us hear the word "apologetics" and panic, thinking, "I need to be prepared with all the answers to all the deep questions." It's certainly not a bad idea to read some apologetics books, but Peter's focus is more on the heart level. You might call it an "apologetics of hope." It's more about adoration than argumentation.

To be an effective witness you need more than a knock-down argument on paper; you need a joyful song in your heart. You need more than logical answers; you need a heart captivated by Jesus. To be a good witness you need to first adore Jesus and be filled with hope. Every Christian can be like this. A new Christian with no formal theological training, for example, can radiate with contagious Christian hope! Evangelism is not for the elite special-forces Christians but for everyone who abounds with gospel hope.

Unbelievers may not grasp your theology, but they can spot your hope (as well as love, joy, and peace). Our hope gets people's attention—so be someone who radiates it in your conduct and your reactions to successes and setbacks, and someone who conveys it in your words. So let's convey that hope as we regularly ponder what Christ has done for us and all that Christ has for us.

It is striking, as you read the Gospels, that in his interactions with people Jesus never used one canned presentation; he knew each person and addressed them individually. As others see our hope and feel their lack of it, their questions get personal. Often our evangelism will feel much more like personal counseling than public proclamation. As unbelievers ask us questions, answer them with gospel clarity and gospel grace.

For as much as what we say matters, how we speak does too. When we commend Christ to others, we need to do so in a Christ-like manner. We must not speak condescendingly or harshly but with "gentleness and respect" (1 Peter 3 v 15). Paul picks up on this in another important passage about our everyday witness:

> *Walk in wisdom toward outsiders, making the best use of the time. Let your speech always be gracious, seasoned with salt, so that you may know how you ought to answer each person. (Colossians 4 v 5-6)*

We are to pay attention to our life and speech around "outsiders" and use our time wisely. God gives you certain golden opportunities to bear witness. Take advantage of them! When you have these opportunities, let your conversation be gracious and winsome.

The phrase "seasoned with salt" is important. New Testament scholar David Garland comments:

> "Seasoned with salt" was used to refer to witty, amusing, clever, humorous speech. Their saltiness will prevent them from being ignored as irrelevant bores … Godliness is not to be equated with stodginess. Flat formulas or lifeless platitudes do not capture the gospel's excitement. It must be made palatable with a savory combination of charm and wit.
>
> (Colossians and Philemon, p 274, 287)

Work to make your witness interesting, lively, and colorful. Avoid boring, tedious, monotonous conversation. Use your personality. Yes, some parts of our personality need to be sanctified, but generally speaking we should share the good news with our personality. If you're quiet, use your natural gentle tone. If you're witty, use your wit. If you're the extroverted social butterfly, let your excitement shine. If you practice hospitality well, let your kindness melt your guests. Every person is interesting because each person is unique! Don't turn into an evangelism robot. Don't preach yourself, but do be yourself.

One of the things that made the gospel so compelling to me in college was the way in which my Christian teammates communicated it to me. It was not boring.

They never gave me a rote presentation. They simply had conversations with me that provoked me to think and ask more questions. They weren't condescending either. They were extremely humble and gracious. Even if I didn't agree with their beliefs, I found them interesting!

May the Lord use our lives to provoke questions as we go about doing good, and may he give us courage to ask good questions as we share the hope of the gospel in a winsome and gentle manner. And, because all people are unique image-bearers of God who are worthy of our attention and care, be ready to answer each person's questions with "salt."

NETWORK EVANGELISM

In years past two primary forms of evangelism have been emphasized: "event" evangelism and "cold call" evangelism. When people hear the word "evangelism" today, they often think of either big events/crusades or door-to-door outreach. While the Lord has used both of these approaches, and sometimes they can still be effective, they are often less fruitful in post-Christian contexts. A third approach, which has historic precedent and which is both culturally appropriate and practically effective, is *network* evangelism.

Network evangelism isn't an event, nor is it a program. It's a lifestyle. It's about living with gospel intentionality within the everyday rhythm of life. It's done among people who fall into one's current web of relationships.

In planting our church, network evangelism became the main way through which we emphasized how every member can do evangelism. We also encouraged teams going out into particular areas to do more cold-call evangelism, but network evangelism has been our main focus, and it has proved very fruitful. Tim Keller's *Church Planting Manual* says that "there must be an atmosphere of expectation that every member will always have 2 to 4 people in the incubator, a force-field in which people are being prayed for, given literature, brought to church or other events" (p 125). We have sought to expand and build on this idea.

Network evangelism has several advantages. *It recognizes the sovereignty of God.* It fosters the belief that every person in our sphere of life matters, and it helps us remember that God has us living in this time and place in history, surrounded by particular image-bearers that he has sovereignly put in our path (Acts 17 v 26-27).

Additionally, *network evangelism has historic precedent.* In his book *Cities of God*, sociologist Rodney Stark describes how it was that Christianity became an urban movement that conquered Rome:

> *Social networks are the basic mechanism through which conversion takes place.... [M]ost conversions are not produced by professional missionaries conveying a new message, but by rank-and-file members who share their faith with their friends and relatives... Although the very first Christian converts in the West may have been*

by full-time missionaries, the conversion process soon became self-sustaining as new converts accepted the obligation to spread their faith and did so by missionizing their immediate circle of intimates. (p 13-14)

Don't miss that! The spread of Christianity in the first century was astonishing—and the movement advanced because Christians accepted the responsibility to spread the gospel within their circle of intimate relationships. *We can do that too, in our day.*

Here is one more benefit: *network evangelism promotes faithfulness and patience in evangelism.* Often, evangelistic methods involve only "on the spot" presentations, and they can be impersonal. They can be about getting numbers, not valuing people. They can simply allow us to check a box to appease our guilt, and then move on. But when you're reaching out to people you see regularly, it requires faithfulness and perseverance. You need to do the necessary pre-evangelism, answer questions, slowly and gradually watch defenses go down, and hopefully— by God's grace—see your friend, family member, co-worker, or neighbor declare, "Jesus is Lord."

ENGAGING WITH PEOPLE IN YOUR NETWORKS

It's helpful to think of your web of relationships in the following five network-categories:

- Familial: people in your family

- Geographical: people in your neighborhood

- Vocational: people at your workplace

- Recreational: people you play with or hang out with

- Commercial: people you see at shops

Try to identify at least five people in each of these networks, and then for each of those people, aim to do at least one of these five tasks. Hopefully, you can do more than one task. Can you pray for them and invite them? Or can you pray for them *and* share the gospel with them? At the very least, you can begin praying for those in your networks. But the goal is to pray, continue praying, and eventually take some further steps.

- *Pray for them.* C.S. Lewis said, "I have two lists of names in my prayers, those for whose conversions I pray and those for whose conversions I give thanks. The little trickle of transferences from List A to List B is a great comfort" (quoted in Phil Ryken, *1 Kings*, p 513). May the Lord give us some of these little trickles of transferences!

- *Invite them.* Have people over for dinner, to play sports, to go to a movie, or to come with you to a church event.

- *Serve them.* Identify a way that you can bless those in your networks. Offer to do childcare, pick up groceries, or do some lawn work for them.

- *Give resources to them.* Ask them to read a book

or article with you, or to listen to a sermon or podcast. This can be a great way to start a gospel conversation.

- *Share the gospel with them.* Look for various points at which you can go deeper into your faith. Remember that you're not the only one commending something or someone to others. Everyone is evangelizing about something: extolling the wonders of aroma therapy, kale smoothies, La Croix, life-changing skin care, Downton Abbey, Busch Gardens, CrossFit, Alexander Hamilton, LeBron for MVP, and more. The gospel is too good, and too important, to keep to ourselves!

Here's a helpful grid to fill in as you think this through—aim to write down five people in each of these five categories, and then for each person do one of these five tasks:

NETWORKS	PEOPLE
Vocational	
Familial	
Geographical	
Commercial	
Recreational/relational	

YOU'RE ALLOWED TO GET HELP

We tend to think of evangelism as an individual exercise, but you can get help from others, particularly as you get to the task of sharing the gospel and answering questions. Evangelize with other members of your church. Some are good at developing relationships; some are good at hospitality; some are good at answering questions.

Evangelism is often a team game. You could be praying for someone you know who is sharing the gospel with a coworker. You might open up your home for an event, but allow someone else to be the event organizer and someone else to be the one who gets a gospel conversation started. When asked a tough question, you might not have the answer, but you could introduce this interested unbeliever to someone who may be able to answer their questions (or go and speak to that person yourself to find out how they would have answered, and then return to restart the conversation with your friend). Think about your own particular spiritual gifts and abilities, and consider how you may do the work of evangelism with other members of your church. This certainly does not mean that you have an excuse never to boldly proclaim the gospel simply because you're uncomfortable with that or because someone else is better at it; but it does mean that you don't have to view evangelism as being exclusively an individual endeavor.

All church members are called to witness to our faith. It is a part of faithfulness. In a post-Christian context, it is also necessary for fruitfulness—we can no longer assume that others can do the evangelism for us. And this is a joy—we should want to be faithful witnesses first and foremost for the glory of God. Whatever the response to our efforts, God is pleased by our faithfulness, and God is glorified by the truth about his Son being uttered in his world. So this is our call: to live a good and faithful life even in the midst of trial and suffering (1 Peter 3 v 17); to respond to questions with the right content and tone; and to always be in our "ready position" to share the hope that we have. Some people may respond in faith to the gospel, while others will not. Some may oppose you. But your call is to be faithful, and to leave the results to God.

ACTION STEPS

Along with taking the time to pray about and then fill in the network-evangelism grid above, here's a useful three-part acronym: NET.

- *N: Never stop praying.* Of all the things you can do for the people in your networks, this is the easiest and one of the best things you can do: pray for them. Identify the people in your networks and begin praying daily for them. Pray quietly as you see them. It's amazing what might open up if we would simply start asking God to bring them to faith in Christ.

- *E: Exercise your faith wisely.* How can you "walk in wisdom toward outsiders"? Be a good employee, live with integrity, and be alert to opportunities when you walk the neighborhood, when you shop, or where you play. Consider giving a book to someone or inviting them to dinner or to a church service. Consider surprising them with an act of service. Think about your context. What would provoke questions from outsiders? Perhaps a book club, or a game night, or involvement in city activities.

- *T: Talk graciously and winsomely.* Commend the gospel in a way that is natural, gentle, and appealing. Treat each person uniquely. Consider thought-provoking questions that you could ask them, or respond to their questions with humility and thoughtfulness. If they disagree with you, do they still enjoy time with you? Carefully consider how Jesus, the friend of sinners, engaged outsiders with the gospel, and pray that you may have that kind of engagement with those far from God.

8. SENDING

CONTINUING THE MISSION AND PLANTING HEALTHY CHURCHES

Our church is young, having been planted about nine years ago. It's not uncommon for people to ask, "How old is your church now?" Because time flies, I have to do some quick math in my head to answer them. To simplify matters, and to teach a bit of church history, I have started responding by saying, "We're over 2,000 years old."

Of course I know what people have in mind when they ask that question (and I do actually answer their question sometimes!), but it's important to keep in mind that the story of "our church" is part of something much bigger. In a sense, it begins in Acts 2, and the story of the church in Acts 2 is *our* history.

The people of God did not originate in the first century—God has always had a people for himself that he has chosen, blessed, and sent out to be a blessing. Nevertheless, the book of Acts marks a pivotal turning point in redemptive history. Acts describes the day of Pentecost, the explosive beginnings of the early church, and the start of the missional history of the church.

Christian, consider what a grand story you are part of! This unfolding story of God gathering a people for himself should encourage you as you look at your local church. Marvel at the faithfulness of God as you consider how the gospel got from Jerusalem to your church and to you. Let your heart be filled with praise—and long for the day in which you join all of our redeemed family from all ages from all around the globe.

CONTINUING THE STORY

We're not only part of the story—we get to continue it and contribute to it. We read of the birth of the church in the 28 chapters of Acts, but the story goes on, and our church and your church are part of that story! Perhaps this is why the book of Acts has such an abrupt ending. Acts 28 closes with a cliffhanger. Paul is ministering in prison, and a bunch of loose ends related to Paul, Peter, the early churches, and more are not tied up. If you were reading a novel with a similar lack of closure, you may be tempted to think that your book is missing a chapter! We're left with the impression that the story is still in progress. And it is! The church today is living out what we might call Acts 29 (which is the reason for the name of the church-planting network that my church is a part of). I don't ordinarily like shows that end with "To be continued..." but this one is exciting because we're part of the story!

Luke didn't intend to write a biography of Paul or anyone else. His purpose was to record the acts of the Lord Jesus through the Holy Spirit. He set out to describe the unstoppable progress of the gospel. His first book, the Gospel of Luke, set out to describe, "all that Jesus began to do and teach until the day when he was taken up" (Acts 1 v 1-2). The book of Acts is about all that Jesus continued to do through the church, now that he has ascended. Jesus is the hero of Acts, not Paul or anyone else. Luke concludes Acts both on a note of victory—with the triumph of the King as Paul preaches his lordship in the capital of the empire—and with the message that while his book is finishing, the mission of Jesus is not.

God replaces the messengers, but the church's message and mission are unchanging until the King returns. Christians today get to enter this redemptive drama! Though we will not add our stories to the Bible, we do get to continue the mission of spreading the good news to the nations. Your church can be a part of that, no less than the churches that we read of in Acts were. So, what does a world-changing local church look like? To catch a glimpse, let's consider the church in Antioch as Luke describes it for us in Acts.

THE ANTIOCH MODEL

Back when we were thinking about what to call our church plant, we considered calling it "Antioch" because I love this church so much. It was a launching pad for worldwide missions. It became a base of operations for Paul's missionary journey with Barnabas (Acts 13 v 1-3;

14 v 26-27), and subsequently a base for his journey with Silas (15 v 35-41; 18 v 22-23).

Antioch was the third largest city in the Greco-Roman world (after Rome and Alexandria), having some 500,000 people. This cosmopolitan city was called "the queen of the East." Politically, it was the capital city of Syria. Geographically, it was located 300 miles north of Jerusalem, and 30 miles east of the Mediterranean Sea, in what is now southeast Turkey. It sat at a crossroads of major highways going to the north, the south, and the east. Greeks, Romans, Syrians, Phoenicians, Jews, Arabs, Egyptians, Africans, Indians, and Asians all populated Antioch, making it remarkably diverse. Religiously, it was very pluralistic and idolatrous. (For more on this, see my book *Exalting Jesus in Acts*, p 156.) In other words, it was in some ways very similar to many places today—multicultural and diverse and full of competing world-views. And like our contexts, it was a great place for a new church! Stott notes, "No more appropriate place could be imagined, either as the venue for the first international church, or as the springboard for the worldwide Christian mission" (*The Message of Acts*, p 203).

What made this outreach to the people in Antioch so powerful? And then what made this new church's witness beyond Antioch so powerful? We can identify several ingredients of a missional church from the story of the origin of the church in Antioch, and from its subsequent outreach to the world.

COMMIT TO CHRIST'S MISSION

When some Christians were scattered as far as Antioch from Jerusalem, some believers spoke the gospel *only* to the Jews (11 v 19). They began where they had connections to family or business. But some men of Cyprus (an island in the Mediterranean) and Cyrene (northern Africa) came to Antioch and preached the good news also to the "Hellenists" or Greek-speaking people (v 20). These courageous and trail-blazing evangelists begin spreading the message of Christ among the Gentile unbelievers. Peter had preached to Cornelius, a Gentile, after receiving a dramatic vision (Acts 10)—but no one had acted strategically and intentionally to preach to the Gentiles yet. And the awakening in Samaria (the region to the north of Jerusalem) in Acts 8 was different too, since the Samaritans were "close cousins to the Jews" (Keller, *Evangelism*, p 98). So here these evangelists were breaking through a major cultural barrier. Despite having Jewish roots, they were committed to engaging the Greeks. Hailing from Cyprus and Cyrene (11 v 20), they wouldn't have had as much of the conservative Palestinian culture in their background as believers from Jerusalem might have had. They wouldn't have had as much anti-Gentile prejudice, and they would have done business with Greeks all the time. So, they were less inflexible than those from Jerusalem.

Why is this important? Because we too cannot withdraw from people if we are to be effective evangelists. We must engage them. An Antioch-like church gets involved with people. We must learn how to live with and speak winsomely to unbelievers.

This explains why these evangelists went about "preaching the Lord Jesus" (v 20). They weren't preaching about Jesus as the "Christ" (though he is!) but about Jesus as "Lord." We don't read here about "Christ Jesus," "Messiah Jesus," or "the anointed King, Jesus." Why? This isn't a Jewish crowd. This is a Gentile crowd, unfamiliar with the promises that God made throughout the Old Testament to send his anointed Messiah-King. Of course they would eventually hear about the Christ and be known as his followers, to the extent that their neighbors would label them as "Christians" (v 26). But you don't get the sense that the evangelists started there. The Gentiles wouldn't have been as interested in "the hope of Israel." But the title *Kurios*, Lord, was commonly spoken in Antioch. These evangelists were able to tell everyone about the Kurios who is the only Lord.

To be good evangelists, you need to know the gospel well, and you need to know the people to whom you're speaking well too. A tract with a little formula for every person in every place is very unlikely to work. You must preach the gospel in a way that is intelligible to the person with whom you're speaking.

Here's something striking about this story: we don't know who these Christians were! Even though this outreach effort in Antioch would change the world, we don't even know the evangelists' names. Unknown Christians really can make a difference, and unknown Christians are never unknown to Christ, whose verdict on us matters most. The most important people in the church aren't always the most recognized. Don't confuse admiration with importance.

As we thought about in the previous chapter, this kind of evangelism—in which we know the gospel and know the people to whom it's being proclaimed—is effective: "And the hand of the Lord was with them, and a great number of people who believed turned to the Lord" (11 v 21). Here's the key: the Lord's hand was on these witnesses as they witnessed faithfully and thoughtfully.

DISCIPLING BELIEVERS
Luke goes on to describe how Barnabas and Saul strengthened these new believers. His description of this discipleship process is also enlightening for us. It involved *accountability*, *instruction*, and *encouragement*.

The church sent Barnabas to check out things in Antioch. Some may have been critical and suspicious of the growth there, but others were probably hopeful and wanted to help encourage this group of new believers in Antioch, who had no apostolic leadership. Further, this would have been a challenging church to lead, given the varying backgrounds and the infancy of the believers' faith. They needed wise pastoral care in order to mature in the faith. So Barnabas came, evaluated, and endorsed the work.

But discipleship requires more than good accountability and oversight; it also involves life-giving encouragement. Barnabas was the right man for this job too! His ministry of encouragement garnered him the nickname "son of encouragement." Instead of being the cold-water committee, in his encouragement Barnabas poured gasoline on the fire.

Moreover, he saw God at work. Luke tells us, "When he … saw the grace of God, he was glad" (11 v 23a). Some see the grace of God and are mad. But grace-loving believers like Barnabas spill over with joy and encouragement. So, don't think lightly of encouragement. This is what the saints needed then, and it is what saints need today. You need good theology to be a disciple-maker, but you also need to be an encourager.

Barnabas needed additional support, so he fetched Saul (Paul), who was in his native city of Tarsus. Barnabas knew of Saul's calling to be an apostle to the Gentiles (9 v 15-16), and he perhaps already knew what would soon become clear to all—that Saul's background gave him the ability to communicate to diverse groups. Barnabas found a world-class mind for this world-reaching congregation. Paul and Barnabas stayed for a whole year (11 v 26). Can you imagine a year with Paul and Barnabas?! Their teaching trained and equipped the believers in Antioch for the important work ahead.

It was now that these new believers in Antioch became known by the name "Christian" (v 26). This was the term that unbelievers used to describe believers. These saints in Antioch (of all places!) so identified with Jesus that fellow Gentile citizens called them "little Christs." Previously, people assumed that Christianity was just some form of Judaism. But now, the Christians were viewed differently than Jews and differently than unconverted Gentiles. They were "Christians." And this third classification included believers from very diverse backgrounds. Today, many people still assume that one's religion is based on one's race, class, or family. But Antioch showed the world something beautifully different. It all stemmed from their wholehearted commitment to Christ, expressed through their evangelism and discipleship.

SHOWING MERCY

The big-heartedness of the Antioch believers shone when a major problem impacted the Roman Empire: famine (v 27-30). A prophet, Agabus, told the Christians that this famine would come. They responded beautifully, especially in their show of support for those in Jerusalem. Everyone gave according to their ability, and they sent the gift by the hands of Barnabas and Saul (v 29-30; 12 v 25).

Mercy ministry (meeting needs through deeds) is a selfless ministry. These Christians had heard about the famine before everyone else did; they could have hoarded supplies for themselves. (If people had known about COVID-19 ahead of time, many would have surely hoarded supplies, as well as invested in Amazon, well before lockdown came!) Instead, the Antioch Christians considered the needs of others.

To reflect the Antioch model, we need to consider the needs of this broken world and give as we have the ability. Hopefully your church has ministries and partnerships that can help you do this, whether it's ministry to the orphan, widow, refugee, prisoner, sick, dying, hungry, oppressed, and more. This kind of generosity shows that the gospel has transformed you (2 Corinthians 8 v 9).

Mercy ministry can be done in your own life as a Christian going about doing good, but it's also important to be part of *corporate* mercy ministry—something in which the entire church participates. In this story, the church in Antioch commits to care for another church. The Jerusalem church was much different in culture and background, and was a long way from Antioch. However, both churches belonged to Jesus, and they were brothers and sisters. The Antioch church gave a tangible expression of this unity through sending their gift.

Missional churches are mindful of the needs of other churches. Recently, during the pandemic, many churches in our Acts 29 network sent financial gifts to the churches that belong to our "Church in Hard Places" group. These like-minded churches exist in some of the most dangerous, most difficult, and poorest places around the world. In the midst of uncertain times, it was a joy to show our support for those who were being impacted by the pandemic in some devastating ways.

PURSUING DIVERSITY

Skipping ahead to Acts 13, you find Luke giving us the names of a diverse group of leaders in this church (Acts 13 v 1). This too is something to pursue in our own churches, for both pastoral and evangelistic purposes.

Barnabas was a Cypriot Jewish believer (4 v 36). Luke doesn't provide the background of Simeon, who was called "Niger," but his name means "black" or "dark." Most believe that he was a black man from Africa. Lucius came from "Cyrene"; that is, North Africa. Manaen, who was brought up in Herod's court, was related to the royal upper class, being either a foster brother or other relative of Herod Antipas. And then there was Saul, who was a Jewish believer. He would have brought an academic, professorial dynamic to the leadership.

So, if you had visited this church, one of the first things that would have caught your attention would have been the diversity of the leaders—and of the members as well. The diverse leadership simply reflected the diverse membership. Such diversity would have been a powerfully attractive scene to the unbelieving Antioch culture. Each citizen could have envisioned themselves as being part of such a people. They would have seen that the good news is not for one particular tribe or group but for all the nations. They could have envisioned these leaders caring for them regardless of their background. It shouldn't surprise us that such a diverse church became the springboard to worldwide missions.

SENDING MISSIONARIES

If a church isn't sending, it's ending. This may sound counter-intuitive, but usually churches that are raising up and sending out missionaries and church planters are vibrant churches. One reason for this is that sending and church planting constantly keeps the mission in front of people in the sending church. Antioch certainly models this to us.

Up to this point in Acts, the gospel had been limited to Palestine/Syria. But all of that changed as the church was worshiping, fasting, and being sensitive to the Spirit, and these gathered believers were led to send Barnabas and Paul on mission (13 v 1-3).

When it comes to sending missionaries and planters, we need to avoid both *individualism* and *institutionalism*. Individualism means Christians act as lone-ranger missionaries. That's not the picture in Acts. The church affirms the missionary calling, and they also provide ongoing support. Institutionalism means a mechanical and bureaucratic process, devoid of prayer and the Spirit's leadership. Instead, we're to learn from the model here: missionaries are directed by the Spirit and sent and supported by the church.

Sending good people out from your church is never easy. Imagine how the believers in Antioch felt—they were sending Barnabas and Paul! This required both sacrifice and faith. Yet they did it as an act of obedience and because the mission is worth it.

Missional churches continue to send their best on mission. It's often painful, but we call these send-offs "gospel goodbyes." We're saying goodbye for the sake of the gospel. As we do, we can remember that we will have billions of years to fellowship with our brothers and sisters. So we say farewell in the short run, and we continue to pray for and support them.

In sending out our best, we should also remember the fact that God sent out his own best—his own Son—for mission. We are reflecting the very nature of our God and following in the footsteps of our Savior when we send or when we go.

PLANTING CHURCHES

As the story of Acts unfolds from this scene in Antioch, we read of ongoing evangelism and church planting. The church in Antioch was a church plant that had a wide reach through planting more churches, and today we need churches which replicate their missional passion.

It's not uncommon for some church members to have little teaching regarding the need to plant churches. I mean, don't we have enough churches? Why start more? What follows is a bit of church planting 101.

First, *we plant churches to align ourselves with the purposes of God*. God has always been committed to gathering a people for himself, not just isolated individual believers who go to heaven (Acts 18 v 9-10). Therefore, when a team plants a church, they're doing more than starting a meeting at a building or in a home. They're taking part in what God has always been doing. They're also getting and giving a foretaste of where history is headed: toward God gathering a diverse, global people to himself.

Second, *we plant churches because the Great Commission points to church planting*. While it's true that we don't read of an explicit command to "plant churches," Jesus did command us "to make disciples of all nations" by "baptizing them" and "teaching them" (Matthew 28 v 18-20). What do you call this discipling of people by baptizing and teaching them? I call it incorporating new believers into the life of a church. Baptism is a public profession of faith which identifies believers with the body of Christ. After Peter preached on the day of Pentecost, people were converted and then baptized (Acts 2 v 41), and immediately these baptized believers then gathered for worship to (among other things) teach all that Jesus commanded (v 42-47). Teaching new baptized believers happens primarily in the local church. I would contend, then, that the Great Commission points us to the idea of church planting—not church planting with a building, a budget, and a website, but church planting in terms of identifying new believers through baptism and in terms of equipping believers in the word.

Third, *the New Testament church was largely a collection of church plants*. Acts tells the story of the explosive growth of new churches; and the epistles show how the apostles provided leadership to these new churches. Read the epistles and ask how these churches got started; you can trace many of them back to the book of Acts. Therefore, church planting is the air we breathe in the God-breathed Bible.

Finally, *Paul's basic ministry methodology was urban church planting*. Over and over, we read how churches in influential cities were established, elders were appointed, and instructions were given to these new congregations (see Acts 14 v 21-23). Indeed, Paul wanted to preach the gospel "not where Christ has already been named" (Romans 15 v 20), and after that evangelism came the establishment of new churches. After churches with sound doctrine and qualified leaders had been established in these major cities, Paul moved on, which is how he could say, "I no longer have any room for work in these regions" (v 23). This wasn't because he had evangelized everyone in the entire region, but because he had helped equip believers through new churches in the major cities of these regions. These churches then spread the gospel to the more rural surrounding areas: how? You guessed it—through preaching the gospel and planting churches of new believers.

These are a few of the biblical reasons why we plant churches. There are other practical considerations as well, like the fact that in societies in which more people are moving the into urban centers, we need more and more churches there! Further, Tim Keller points out some other practical reasons for church planting, which may apply to a variety of contexts: first, younger adults are disproportionately found in new congregations; second, newer congregations reach new residents better; and third, new social groups are better reached by new congregations (*Church Planting Manual*, p 29).

All this is to say that a church member needs to be committed to sending: sending gifts, sending people, sending church-plant groups to start up new communities of light scattered across the earth, for the good of the world and for the glory of God. It's a mission that requires sacrifice from both the senders and the sent; but it's a mission more than worthy of sacrifice—and it's a mission in which every church member is called to participate.

ACTION STEPS
As you think about your role as a member of a missional church, here are some further action steps to consider.

- *Adopt a cultural-engagement mentality.* To be faithful witnesses, we cannot have a "bomb shelter mentality," but rather we need to adopt a mentality that faithfully communicates the good news with others. Pray for the Lord to give you wisdom and boldness as you seek to reach people from all kinds of backgrounds.

- *Encourage those who are engaging in faithful evangelism and mission.* Be a Barnabas! When you see the Lord working through fellow believers, rejoice in it, and speak words of life-giving encouragement to these saints.

- *Meditate much on the mercy and grace of Christ toward you, and let this motivate you to do mercy ministry.* Generous and sacrificial mercy ministry flows from a heart that's free from the world's vices and that's captivated by the Savior's victory.

- *Get involved in church planting by praying, giving, supporting, or going.* Don't underestimate the importance of prayer for church planting! And realize that your financial contribution and ongoing support are greatly needed. As you pray, give, and support, remain open to the Spirit's direction in your own life. He may lead you into the privilege of being part of a church-planting team yourself.

CONCLUSION

A VISION OF YOUR CHURCH

Hopefully this book has given you a vision of what the church is and why you should invest your life in a local body of believers—and how you can do that.

It's easy to drive by church buildings on Sundays and not think much about what's happening there. Of course (and tragically), some are lifeless places with little gospel or Spirit—but where they contain a group of believers who are preaching the gospel and displaying the marks of a faithful church, more is happening than most people (including its members) realize. A church may appear irrelevant and weak. But what we sometimes fail to consider is that the church is at the heart of God's plan for the world. We fail to remember what Christ did to have a bride for himself, and we fail to consider how the church points to the future. It is not just outsiders who do not appreciate the wonder of the church; it's also easy for us Christians to fail to consider how awesome it is to be a living stone in the temple of the Lord.

So let me leave you with John's inspiring vision of the future—of our future:

Then I saw in the right hand of him who was seated
on the throne a scroll written within and on the back,
sealed with seven seals. And I saw a mighty angel
proclaiming with a loud voice, "Who is worthy to open
the scroll and break its seals?" And no one in heaven or
on earth or under the earth was able to open the scroll
or to look into it, and I began to weep loudly because
no one was found worthy to open the scroll or to look
into it. And one of the elders said to me, "Weep no
more; behold, the Lion of the tribe of Judah, the Root of
David, has conquered, so that he can open the scroll and
its seven seals."

And between the throne and the four living creatures
and among the elders I saw a Lamb standing, as though
it had been slain, with seven horns and with seven eyes,
which are the seven spirits of God sent out into all the
earth. And he went and took the scroll from the right
hand of him who was seated on the throne. And when
he had taken the scroll, the four living creatures and
the twenty-four elders fell down before the Lamb, each
holding a harp, and golden bowls full of incense, which
are the prayers of the saints. And they sang a new song,
saying,

"Worthy are you to take the scroll
  and to open its seals,

> *for you were slain, and by your blood you ransomed*
> *people for God*
> *from every tribe and language and people and nation,*
> *and you have made them a kingdom and priests to*
> *our God,*
> *and they shall reign on the earth."*
>
> *(Revelation 5 v 1-10)*

When your church gathers together to praise our Redeemer, you are getting a foretaste of this coming glory. Future reality is breaking into the present in your local church.

When I cook a meal, I'm usually grilling outside. And often, I will take a bite of the steak or chicken or fish to sample it. That little bite is but a foretaste of the glory of the meal to come. And it's like that in the life of our local church. Our local church gives us a little taste of heaven.

One day we will be gathered with the redeemed, singing praise to the Lamb, who was slain for sinners. "Are all of these people our family?" we might ask. "Yes," those around us will answer, "these brothers and sisters are our family, and all because of the work of our Savior." We're following the Lamb into the new creation together, where we will experience total peace, complete healing, and unspeakable joy in his presence. And God has given you your church to be the place where you sample that reality; where you are formed to be more and more like our Savior as you are reminded in his word and in baptism and the Lord's Supper of what he has done for you; where you respond to his love in song and prayer and service; where you find family who can share your joys and walk with you through your valleys. It is an awesome thing to be a member of a local church, and it is a wonderful thing to know that our prayers and our efforts can make a difference not only today, but for eternity. So, pursue faithfulness to Christ and his church today. Belong, welcome, gather, care, serve, honor, witness, and send. The Lord of the church loves you with an undying love. So, love your church.

DISCUSSION GUIDE

1. BELONGING

Read Ephesians 2 v 18 – 3 v 19

1. What images does Paul use to describe the church in 2 v 18-22? What does he want us to see about the church's identity?

2. Paul's mission is to preach to the Gentiles. What is his ultimate purpose, and the purpose of the church (3 v 1-13)?

3. What does Paul pray for his readers (v 14-19)? Why do you think he includes the phrase "together with all the Lord's holy people"—and how does that change your understanding of his prayer?

4. In your church, what does it look like to commit and belong? How could you encourage one another to do this? What rewards do you hope to reap?

5. What's the danger in not belonging to a specific local congregation?

6. What will you pray for your church, based on this passage?

2. WELCOMING

Read James 2 v 1-13

1. How does James show that favoritism is not just unhelpful but wrong (v 4-7)?

2. Why is it such a serious thing to do (v 8-13)?

3. Why does favoritism dishonor not only other people but God himself? And conversely, why is acting without partiality a reflection of God's own character and actions?

4. What types of favoritism are particularly tempting in your setting? What are you and your church most likely to discriminate on the basis of?

5. In what ways is your church strong at welcoming outsiders? Where could it improve?

6. How can you personally be a part of that? What might need to change about the way you act or speak, both at church gatherings and during the week?

3. GATHERING

Read Hebrews 12 v 18-29

1. The author of Hebrews is comparing the moment when the Israelites gathered at Mount Sinai (v 18-21) to the state of affairs now (v 22-24). What's different and why? How does this serve as a motivation to gather as a church?

2. The description of verses 22-24 is in one sense looking to the future gathering of all God's people in heaven. But it's also describing something of what happens in our gatherings now. Who are we gathering with? How should that impact the way we think about our Sunday meetings?

3. Why is it so urgent to listen to God's voice and to worship him together (v 25-29)?

4. On a Sunday, do you think of yourself as being there to contribute to and build up others in your congregation? How could you do this more?

5. What aspects of church gatherings do you personally find most precious? Why is it so valuable to gather to hear God's word, share the Lord's Supper, sing, and pray together?

6. What could you do to prepare well for Sunday? What "holy and happy habits" could you build, and how could that make a difference to your experience of corporate worship?

4. CARING

Read Galatians 5 v 16 – 6 v 10

1. In 5 v 16-25, what reasons does Paul give for doing good to one another? What makes it possible to be caring and not selfish?

2. What dangers might we fall into as we seek to care for one another (6 v 1, 3-4, 9)? What ideas do you have on how you can avoid those while not holding back on caring for others?

3. What is our aim and ultimate hope as we do good to one another? How does this help us to persevere?

4. What is the greatest challenge in these verses for you personally?

5. Is your church one in which restoring, burden-bearing, sharing, and doing good take place? Which one is your weak point? What could you do to step up in that area?

6. What steps could you take to educate or train yourself (whether personally or as a congregation) in how to care for others effectively?

5. SERVING

Read Romans 12 v 1-21

1. What does whole-life worship look like, and what motivates it (v 1-2)?

2. How should we see our own identity (v 5)? How does this help us to serve well?

3. Verses 9-21 contain some challenging instructions. Why is doing these things hard? What difference can they make (v 21)?

4. What gifts has God given you? How can you use them with excellence, passion, and humility for the good of your church?

5. What needs do you see in your church? How could you meet them?

6. Is there anything in Paul's instructions that is lacking in your church's life or in your own life? How will you pray in response to this passage?

6. HONORING

Read 1 Peter 5 v 1-5

1. What dangers does Peter want his readers to avoid— both elders and other members of the church?

2. What is the purpose of elders and pastors seeking to lead in the way Peter instructs?

3. What is the purpose of church members being "subject to the elders"?

4. In what areas might people find it especially hard to submit to their elders? Have you had experiences of this kind of tension in church? What would humility, respect, and love look like in those situations?

5. In what ways are your elders and pastors a good example to you? How could you follow their example?

6. What might encourage each of your elders and pastors this week? How could you help them keep in mind Peter's vision for leadership? What will you pray for them?

7. WITNESSING

Read 1 Peter 3 v 13-17

1. Why do you think honoring and revering Christ (v 15) makes it easier to avoid fearing others (v 14)?

2. What results should there be from doing good (v 13, 14, 16)?

3. As we engage with others, why is it important both to articulate a reason for our hope and to speak with gentleness and respect, as verse 15 directs us to?

4. Are you full of hope? What can you do to cultivate this virtue? How would you explain the reason for it?

5. What does it look like to speak with "gentleness and respect"? In what kinds of relationships is doing so particularly easy or particularly challenging? How can you help one another to grow in this area?

6. In what ways are you currently pursuing obedience to the call to make disciples (Matthew 28 v 19) both individually, as a group, and as a whole church? How could you be most effective as witnesses to your particular community?

8. SENDING

Read Acts 11 v 19-30; 13 v 1-3

1. How do we see God at work through people as the Antioch church is established (11 v 19-25)?

2. What different roles do Barnabas and Saul play?

3. What attitude do the Antioch Christians have toward other churches, toward Saul and Barnabas, toward unreached people, and toward God himself? What does this teach you as a local church today?

4. How outward-looking are you as a church? What would be one step you could take to grow in this area together?

5. In your church, what could you do to follow the example of Barnabas? How could you encourage others to do the same?

6. What will you pray for your church, your community, and the world in the light of this passage?

BIBLIOGRAPHY

Gregg R. Allison, *Sojourners and Strangers* (Crossway, 2012)

Thabiti Anyabwile, *What Is a Healthy Church Member?* (Crossway, 2008)

Michael F. Bird, *Romans* in The Story of God Bible Commentary series (Zondervan, 2016)

Dietrich Bonhoeffer, *Life Together* (Harper One, 1954)

F.F. Bruce, *The Book of Acts* in The New International Commentary on the New Testament series (Eerdmans, 1988)

Tim Chester, *Stott on the Christian Life* (Crossway, 2020)

Mark Dever, "The Church" in *A Theology of the Church,* ed. Daniel L. Akin (B&H, 2007)

Mark Dever, *Nine Marks of a Healthy Church* (Crossway, 2000)

Gordon Fee, *The First Epistle to the Corinthians* in The New International Commentary on the New Testament series (revised edition: Eerdmans, 2014)

David Garland, *Colossians and Philemon* in the NIV Application Commentary series (Zondervan, 1998)

Timothy J. Keller and J. Allen Thompson, *Church Planting Manual* (Redeemer Church Planting Center, 2002)

Timothy Keller, *Galatians for You* (The Good Book Company, 2013)

Timothy Keller, *Romans 8 – 16 For You* (The Good Book Company, 2016)

Timothy Keller, *Evangelism: Studies in the Book of Acts* (Redeemer Presbyterian Church, 1996)

D. Martyn Lloyd-Jones, *Spiritual Depression* (Eerdmans, 1965)

Tony Merida, *Exalting Jesus in Acts* (B&H, 2017)

Douglas J. Moo, *The Letter of James* in The Pillar New Testament Commentary series (Eerdmans, 2000)

James Paton, ed., *The Story of John G. Paton* (Hodder and Stoughton, 1984)

Philip Ryken, *1 Kings* in the Reformed Expository Commentary series (P&R, 2011)

Philip Ryken, *Galatians* in the Reformed Expository Commentary series (P&R, 2005)

Francis Schaeffer, *The Church at the End of the Twentieth Century* (Downers Grove, 1970)

Rodney Stark, *Cities of God* (Harper One, 2006)

John R.W. Stott, *The Message of Acts* in the Bible Speaks Today series (InterVarsity Press USA, 1990)

John R.W. Stott, *The Message of Galatians* in the Bible Speaks Today series (InterVarsity Press USA, 1968)

Tim Witmer, *The Shepherd Leader* (P&R, 2010)

ACKNOWLEDGMENTS

Thank you to Imago Dei Church. This year marks the tenth anniversary of our existence. We have grown from a small church-plant core team to a vibrant congregation. As Paul said to the Philippians, "You are my joy and crown" (Philippians 4:1). Thanks to the elders of Imago Dei. I could not ask for a better team of pastors. It's a privilege to shepherd the flock with you, and I'm grateful that you not only encourage me to write but enable me to do so.

Thank you to Amber Bowen, Amy Tyson, and Christy Britton. Your thoughtful feedback and insightful edits helped sharpen this book. You're a blessing to me and to my family.

A very special thank you to the amazing editors at The Good Book Company. I'm grateful for your careful editing of this document; you're a great team to work with and I'm honored that you've given me the opportunity to write on this topic that's so dear to my heart.

Thank you, Kimberly, my bride, ally, and dear companion. Our marriage and partnership in ministry is evidence of God's grace. May God strengthen us for many more years of faithful ministry.

Finally, I must "Give thanks to the LORD, for he is good; his faithful love endures forever" (Psalm 107:1). You've given me a deep love for your church and the grace to serve her for your glory.

thegoodbook

C O M P A N Y

BIBLICAL | RELEVANT | ACCESSIBLE

At The Good Book Company, we are dedicated to helping Christians and local churches grow. We believe that God's growth process always starts with hearing clearly what he has said to us through his timeless word—the Bible.

Ever since we opened our doors in 1991, we have been striving to produce Bible-based resources that bring glory to God. We have grown to become an international provider of user-friendly resources to the Christian community, with believers of all backgrounds and denominations using our books, Bible studies, devotionals, evangelistic resources, and DVD-based courses.

We want to equip ordinary Christians to live for Christ day by day, and churches to grow in their knowledge of God, their love for one another, and the effectiveness of their outreach.

Call us for a discussion of your needs or visit one of our local websites for more information on the resources and services we provide.

Your friends at The Good Book Company

thegoodbook.com | thegoodbook.co.uk
thegoodbook.com.au | thegoodbook.co.nz
thegoodbook.co.in